REIKI

# REIKI

*The essential guide to
the ancient healing art*

Chris and Penny Parkes
of The Reiki School

VERMILION
London

1 3 5 7 9 10 8 6 4 2

Text © Penny Parkes 1998
Illustrations © Random House UK Limited 1998

First published in the United Kingdom in 1998 by Vermilion
an imprint of Ebury Press
Random House
20 Vauxhall Bridge Road
London SW1V 2SA

Random House Australia (Pty) Limited
20 Alfred Street, Milsons Point, Sydney,
New South Wales 2061, Australia

Random House New Zealand Limited
18 Poland Road, Glenfield,
Auckland 10, New Zealand

Random House South Africa (Pty) Limited
Endulini, 5A Jubilee Road
Parktown 2193, South Africa

Random House UK Limited Reg. No. 954009

A CIP catalogue record for this book is available from the British Library

ISBN: 0 09 181643 2

Printed and bound in Great Britain by Mackays of Chatham plc, Kent

Although every effort has been made to ensure that the contents
of this book are accurate, it must not be treated as a substitute
for qualified medical advice. Always consult a qualified medical
practitioner. Neither the Author nor the Publisher can be held
responsible for any loss or claim arising out of the use, or misuse,
of the suggestions made or the failure to take medical advice.

# CONTENTS

# PREFACE

We were drawn to Reiki shortly after the death of Chris's parents. We both felt we would have liked to have done much more to relieve their suffering during the last few months of their lives. We decided to take Reiki training for both our own self healing and in the hope that we would be able to help others too.

By the time we had taken First Degree Reiki, the cancer that was spreading through my mother's body had advanced rapidly. Her vibrant, colourful, positive character shone through her eyes, although her body had become very frail.

On one particular day, I noticed her parchment-like skin had become almost translucent as we wrapped her fragile frame in a warm blanket, put on some soft music and began to give her what had become a daily Reiki treatment.

At the end of the treatment her face was animated and she began to describe an incredible vision she had experienced during the treatment. Prior to this time, my mother had always considered herself to be pragmatic and rational, drawn to the tangible rather than the ethereal. She was astonished to find herself describing with some conviction, an experience that once she would have considered to be unreal.

Opposite the bed my mother lay on that day, there was a walk-in wardrobe room. The door was closed. She recounted that during the Reiki treatment she had become aware of a beautiful light streaming through the open door and seeing several brilliantly lit figures gently walking into her room. One of these figures was her late husband. She was almost overcome with emotion. The beings of light communicated to her that she need have no fear, that when the time came for her to leave her body, they would be there for her and an incredible experience awaited her. My mother told us she had never experienced such a vivid dream and described feeling filled with awe and tranquillity.

It was as if from that moment she was transformed. All fear and uncertainty had left her. She was filled with peace. Over the next few days, although she was weak, she put her affairs in order and had meaningful conversations with all close family members and certain friends.

My mother took the extraordinary step of preparing her large family for her impending death. Tissues were in short supply as this remarkable woman simply announced that it would all be over in approximately two weeks and that it was not the end, but a new beginning for us all. Her prediction was correct and her death was incredibly peaceful.

What a contrast this was to the final weeks in the lives of Chris's parents a year or so previously. They had both passed away within 10 months of each other. We had searched then for a better way to help relieve the discomfort, distress and fear they were clearly experiencing.

By the time my mother died, Chris and I knew that Reiki was something we wanted to do for the rest of our lives. This book is dedicated to the memory of my Mother as well as my Father and the memory of Chris's parents who collectively taught us so much.

Penny Parkes

# PART ONE

# REIKI – UNIVERSAL LIFE FORCE ENERGY

# CHAPTER ONE
# WHAT IS REIKI?

The word Reiki means 'universal life force energy'. It refers to an ancient hands-on healing art that was rediscovered and revived in the middle of the nineteenth century by Dr Mikao Usui in Japan. The word Reiki itself is made up of two parts. The syllable 'rei' (rey) describes the universal aspect of this energy and 'ki' (kee) refers to the life force energy that flows through all living things. For thousands of years, numerous cultures, races and religions have been aware of the existence of a life force energy that corresponds to the meaning of 'ki'. It is known as 'chi' by the Chinese, 'prana' by the Hindus, 'baraka' by Sufi's, 'light' by Christians and it is highly likely that it was known as 'ka' by ancient Egyptians.

Many ancient cultures have handed down knowledge of hands-on healing methods throughout history and have referred to the transference of a universal life force energy to promote well-being. Thousands of years ago, the ancient Tibetans had a profound understanding of the nature of matter and energy and used this awareness to heal their bodies, promote inner harmony and guide their spirits to an experience of wholeness and balance.

Later, such healing techniques were to emerge in India. Variations of it are also rooted in Chinese, Japanese, Greek, Roman, Egyptian, Native American and other ancient cultures. Knowledge of such healing arts was carefully guarded and preserved by many ancient cultures. Methods were handed down by word of mouth usually to priests or spiritual leaders and the knowledge was known in its entirety by very few people.

The knowledge of Reiki may not have emerged at all had it not been for the persistence of a Dr Mikao Usui whose research led to the recovery of this ancient healing tradition at the end of the nineteenth century.

## Everything is Energy

The scientific world has known for many years what metaphysical and spiritual teachers have known for centuries. Our physical

13

universe is not composed of any matter at all: it's basic component is a kind of force which could be called energy.

Seemingly solid items as perceived by our physical senses such as a chair or a table appear solid and separate from each other. On finer subatomic levels however, such seemingly solid matter is made up of particles of energy. These particles vibrate at different speeds and it is this speed which holds the pattern of their physical form. Physicists describe particles not as isolated grains of matter but as interconnections in an inseparable cosmic web that interact with each other.

Physically we are all energy. Everything within and around us is made up of energy and we are all part of one great energy field. In *The Tao of Physics*, author Fritjof Capra says:

'The exploration of the subatomic world in the 20th century has revealed the intrinsically dynamic nature of matter. It has shown that the constituents of atoms, the subatomic particles, are dynamic patterns which do not exist as isolated entities, but as integral parts of an inseparable network of interactions. These interactions involve a ceaseless flow of energy manifesting itself as the exchange of particles; a dynamic interplay in which particles are created and destroyed without end in a continual variation of energy patterns. The particle interactions give rise to the stable structures which build up the material world, which again do not remain static, but oscillate in rhythmic movements. The whole universe is thus engaged in endless motion and activity; in a continual cosmic "dance of energy".'

Gary Zukav in *The Dancing Wu Li Masters* says: 'Quantum mechanics view subatomic particles as "tendencies to exist" or "tendencies to happen".' Such particles or patterns of energy have many different forms. Thoughts for example are a very fine, light form of energy, easily and quickly changed. Human tissue is a lighter form of energy, influenced by many elements and changes relatively quickly. A boulder is a denser form, slower to change and yet still affected by finer, lighter forms of energy such as water for example and is changed over a longer period of time. All forms of energy are interrelated and can effect one another.

Quantum physics suggests the fabric of the universe is a form of energy and that all living beings are part of this field of energy. Gary Zukav writes:

> 'the philosophical implication of quantum mechanics is that all of the things in our universe (including us) that appear to exist independently are actually part of one all-encompassing organic pattern and that no parts of that pattern are really separate from it or from each other.'

As well as being composed of energy, it is believed that we also have energy running through us. Many forms of medicine that originate in the East believe that it is this flow of energy that sustains life itself and this leaves the physical body at the time of death. This universal life force energy is said to pass through our systems via channels which orientals call the meridians of the body. In Chinese medicine, the aim of acupuncture is to stimulate the flow of energy through these pathways.

In optimum conditions, it is believed that such vital energy may flow unimpeded through our bodies and we are able to experience good health and inner harmony. Conversely, during periods of stress or tension, it is reduced. This is when we usually experience pain, discomfort or distress. In the Chinese view, health is also affected by the interplay of two polar forces known as 'yin' and 'yang'. These represent cyclical patterns of motion and change. Yin represents the strong male, creative power and yang the female, receptive, maternal element. Disruption in the balance between these two forces is said to result in ill health. Balance between yin and yang is maintained by the continuous flow of energy through the body via the energetic grid or meridians. Should the flow of energy be restricted or blocked, well-being is affected.

Rather like the drain blockages dispersed by proprietary cleaners on television advertisements, Reiki is said to dissolve such energy blocks by dissipating immobilized or slow-moving energy. The energy becomes drawn to the areas where the flow is slowed down or restricted and gently starts to break down the blockage. Gradually this life force energy is encouraged to flow freely again and help restore inner balance once more.

Particles of energy appear to be self directing. Interestingly, Reiki energy does not need directing by the person giving the treatment. Gary Zukav describes:

'The astounding discovery awaiting newcomers to physics is that the evidence gathered in the development of quantum mechanics indicates that subatomic "particles" continuously appear to be making decisions! More than that, the decisions they make are based on decisions made elsewhere. Subatomic particles seem to know instantaneously what decisions are made elsewhere and elsewhere can be as far away as another galaxy! The key word is instantaneously! How can a subatomic particle over here know what decision another particle over there has made at the same time the particle over there makes it?'

## Reiki Attunements

The key to Reiki and one of the main differences between this and other healing modalities is the attunement process, the catalyst for amplifying the life force energy.

### What is an Attunement?

An attunement is a procedure in which the Reiki Master or teacher uses symbols and mantras to create a strengthened connection between the person and the universal life force energy. A series of attunements given by a suitably qualified Reiki Master are essential in order to become a channel for the energy.

Dr Usui, the founder, discovered how to use this energy as a beneficial healing treatment for others by using the attunements as a technique, which awakens and amplifies the life force energy in anyone who has the desire to learn, so that they can become a recipient or a channel for the energy. He developed a system so simple that even a child could quickly learn to use it.

This increase in life force energy is brought about as a result of a series of attunements which 'fine tune' the energy field of the recipient. This allows an increased flow of this energy through that person's system for the rest of their life.

Subsequently, it is possible to use the energy for self-treatment as well as being able to treat others. Reiki accelerates the healing process by supporting the body's natural ability to heal itself. As well as being a powerful tool for self healing, Reiki can be used to treat others. Additionally pets, plants and any living thing can benefit too.

# CHAPTER TWO
# THE HISTORY OF REIKI'S USUI SYSTEM

The latter part of the 1800s was a transformational period in Japan's history and many changes were occurring throughout Japanese society. It was towards the end of the nineteenth century that Dr Mikao Usui, then the Dean of a small Christian University in Kyoto was asked by students whether he believed that biblical stories were factual. Affirming that he did, he was then asked whether he believed in Christ's power to heal and whether it was possible to demonstrate this phenomenon. Dr Usui told students that whilst believing in it, he was simply unable to demonstrate it or prove that such a phenomena had ever existed.

This question intrigued Dr Usui to such a degree that it led to his resignation whereupon he left Japan to undertake research into this field. This was ultimately to become his life's quest.

Usui had been taught by a number of Christian missionaries and he therefore decided to begin his research in a Christian society. He studied initially for seven years at the University of Chicago achieving a Doctorate in theology though failing to uncover any data that advanced his research. He eventually turned his attention to Buddhism. He returned to Japan to see if he could uncover information about Buddha's healings.

Dr Usui visited several monasteries but failed to uncover any records. His research was discouraged by Abbots who told him that current emphasis centred on 'healing the spirit' rather than on physical healing.

Usui's determination eventually led him to a Zen monastery where he was encouraged by the Abbott and offered a base from which to continue his studies. Inspired by this Abbott's enthusiasm, Dr Usui remained with the monastery for a considerable period of time where he studied the Sutras in Japanese but uncovered little to advance his research.

Eventually, Dr Usui began an in-depth study of Chinese, which led to him studying the Sutras of Tibet, for which a

*Dr Usui*

knowledge of Sanskrit was necessary. After some time, he was said to have made a trip to Northern India and possibly also to Tibet. He may have studied Tibetan scrolls found during the nineteenth century documenting the travels of St Isa, whom several scholars believe to have been Jesus.

Whether Usui studied these ancient scrolls or other scrolls is not known, but it is believed that he had found some answers in the Japanese Sutras written about Buddha. He also uncovered some writings by an unknown student of Buddha's, which outlined a method by which Buddha was able to heal. Usui was however unable to make this technique work. Though unable to empower the formula, Usui felt he had now found the key.

Believing he was somehow closer to finding the answers he sought, Dr Usui returned to the Zen monastery in Kyoto, Japan and sought advice from the Abbott. It was agreed that following some 14 years of research, the next step would be to undertake a mountain retreat where he could fast and meditate, rather in the style of the Native American 'Vision Quest'.

Dr Usui set out to climb a sacred mountain about 17 miles from Kyoto, Mount Kuri Yama. He reached a specific eastern facing point where accompanied only by 21 stones to act as his calendar, he began his retreat and meditation.

After 20 days of meditation, nothing out of the ordinary had occurred. Just before the predawn on the 21st day, Usui saw a flicker of light appear in the darkness. This light began to move very quickly towards him. As it grew larger, Usui began to feel frightened. His immediate impulse was to retreat, but feeling that this could be some sort of sign or even the answer he had been waiting for, he decided not to move and braced himself for whatever was to come. The light quickly came closer and closer to him until it struck him in the centre of his forehead.

Usui later recounted that he thought he had died. A vision of millions of rainbow-coloured bubbles appeared before his eyes. These became white glowing bubbles each one containing a three-dimensional Sanskrit character in gold. They would appear one by one, just slowly enough for him to register each character. Finally the vision faded. Usui awoke from what had been a trance-like state surprised to find that it was now extremely, bright daylight.

He decided to quickly make his descent down the mountain

to relay the occurrence to his friend the Abbot at the Zen monastery. He was astonished to find he felt extraordinarily well despite his fast and understood that there had been some sort of inner transformation, as a result of the vision.

During his hasty descent, Dr Usui injured his toe. Instinctively he placed his hand on the injured area for a few moments. When he lifted his hand off, he was astonished to find that bleeding had stopped and the pain had subsided. A remarkable transformation had taken place. He continued on his journey and later stopped for refreshments at an inn lower down the mountain. He noticed the daughter of the innkeeper was in great pain with toothache. The location of the inn was remote and it was several day's journey away from the nearest town. Asking permission to place his hands over the painful area, Dr Usui found that the pain and swelling rapidly diminished, much to the delight and relief of the innkeeper's daughter. Dr Usui realised that a second miracle had occurred that day.

On his return to the monastery, Dr Usui discovered the Abbott suffering from arthritis. Again, Dr. Usui found he was able to relieve the discomfort by placing his hands over the painful areas. The Abbott was delighted and amazed by Dr Usui's experience and transformation.

Now he had this knowledge and ability, Dr Usui wanted to determine the best way of using it to help others. He decided to begin work in the beggars' quarters of Kyoto, where he could help a great number of disadvantaged people who were experiencing considerable hardship and suffering. He was subsequently to spend several years in the beggars' quarter, where he was reported to have healed and helped numerous people.

Hoping for their successful reintegration into society, Dr Usui was later distraught to find that after several years, those who had been healed and had gone on to find jobs in the city, were beginning to reappear in the beggars' quarters. Devastated, he realized that he may well have been healing the physical and not the spirit as the Abbots of the other monasteries had earlier emphasised. He began to appreciate that he had failed to teach them responsibility for themselves. He also realized that healing of the spirit was every bit as important as healing the physical body.

By giving Reiki away he reinforced their sense of helplessness.

People needed to give back something for what they received or life would be valueless. It was necessary to have *an exchange of energy.*

Dr Usui then went on to develop the system of healing as we know it today. Drawing on the symbols, he began to teach Reiki all over Japan. He introduced five ethical principles (See Chapter 10) and taught self-treatment and the treatment of others.

### The Five Principles of Reiki

Just for today, do not worry
Just for today, do not anger
Honour your parents, teachers and elders
Earn your living honestly
Show gratitude to every living thing

He also began to train other teachers. One of these was a retired naval officer called Dr Chujiro Hayashi who had worked with Dr Usui for a considerable period of time. It was during the early 1920s, that Dr Usui handed over the knowledge and responsibility of carrying on the Reiki tradition to Dr Hayashi. It is not known why Dr Hawashi was selected. It is believed that Dr Usui was honoured by the Emperor of Japan for his good deeds before his death on March 9th, 1926.

Dr Hayashi treated many people, taught Reiki and founded a Reiki clinic in Tokyo. It was here that a Japanese American woman from Hawaii appeared in 1935. Mrs Hawayo Takata was a widow with two young children suffering from depression plus a number of organic disorders. It was through Mrs Takata, that Reiki was to eventually come to the West.

Mrs Takata was on the verge of surgery when she heard the voice of her late husband discouraging her from having the operation and urging her to find 'another way'. She wondered initially if she was also losing her mind, hearing voices. When the voice repeated itself three times, she decided to ask the doctor who was treating her if there was another way. He happened to have a family member who had been treated successfully at the Reiki clinic close to the hospital and suggested that treatment there could certainly be an alternative option.

Mrs Takata presented herself there for treatment. Initially very sceptical about such a hands-on therapy, she found herself

*Dr Hayashi*

*Mrs Takata*

*Ms Furumoto*

becoming gradually more intrigued by this method of healing. She was treated by several practitioners at one time and noticed how hot their hands became. At one stage she was convinced of trickery on their part and grabbed at the sleeves of their kimonos to try to expose whatever must be generating all this heat. She found nothing and after being reassured by Dr Hayashi, she relaxed greatly. After several months of treatment, to her own astonishment, Mrs Takata was healed.

Understandably impressed, Mrs Takata was very keen to learn Reiki and bring it back to Hawaii. In the male-dominated Japanese society of that era, Mrs Takata met with considerable opposition. She was determined and her persistence paid off. Dr Hayashi took her on as an apprentice and she lived with his family learning and practising Reiki for over a year. She was eventually initiated into First and Second Degree Reiki and she later returned to Hawaii where she began to practise. In 1938, Dr Hayashi initiated Mrs Takata as a Reiki Master enabling her to teach and attune others to Reiki.

It was some time after Dr Hayashi had returned to Japan that Mrs Takata had a powerful dream that caused her great concern. She knew she had to return to Japan to be with Dr Hayashi. Dr Hayashi was a powerful psychic and discussed the implications of the impending war between Japan and the United States with Mrs Takata. He also foresaw the outcome. In this context, he passed on the entire knowledge of Reiki to Mrs Takata and warned of the preparations she would need to make to ensure her own safety and to protect the Reiki heritage.

Dr Hayashi died shortly after this, prior to the outbreak of war. Mrs Takata subsequently returned to Hawaii where she set up a clinic and continued her practise of Reiki. After the war, Reiki was lost to Japan and Mrs Takata became the sole bearer of this knowledge. She was to continue with her practise of Reiki for another 40 years though it was not until the 1970s that she began to train other teachers. She died on December 12th, 1980 having enabled more than twenty others to become Reiki Masters.

On her death, the task of heading the Usui System of Reiki was given to both her granddaughter, Phyllis Lei Furumoto and another Master, Dr Barbara Weber Ray. They worked together for about a year and then parted for personal reasons.

Over twenty of the Masters initiated by Mrs Takata subsequently elected Ms. Furumoto as the successor and Grand Master of the Usui System of Reiki. They formed the Reiki Alliance to both honour the spiritual lineage of the Usui System of Reiki and standardize the way in which it was taught. The Reiki Alliance today has offices in the USA and Europe. Dr Ray formed her own organization and developed the system in a different way which she later named the Radiance Technique.

Until the spring of 1988, only the Grand Master initiated students as Reiki Masters. Ms Furumoto subsequently gave all Masters permission to train and initiate others into the Third Degree. The Usui System of Reiki subsequently spread to Europe and many other countries of the world.

The Usui Masters acknowledge the form as taught by Mrs Takata and Phyllis Lei Furumoto and it is practised unchanged today. This form has nine elements, all of equal importance. If any one of the nine elements is significantly altered or missed out, the system is no longer the Usui System. The nine elements of this form are initiations, money, symbols, treatments, oral tradition, spiritual lineage, history and the five principles.

In April 1992, Paul David Mitchell became the Head of the Discipline and he works closely with Phyllis Furumoto to further clarify the form of the Usui System of Reiki. At the time of writing, they both offer training and guidance to Masters in many parts of the world, mainly on the elements of this form, to ensure that training conforms to defined standards. (To contact Phyllis Furumoto and Paul Mitchell see Office of the Grand Master in the list of addresses at the back of the book).

# CHAPTER THREE
# HOW REIKI DIFFERS FROM OTHER HEALING METHODS

One of the ways in which Reiki differs from other healing methods is in the attunement or initiation process. Attunements are specific procedures (based on symbols and various techniques) carried out by Reiki Masters which increase the individual's capacity to allow a greater amount of universal life force energy to pass through them. A channel is created in each attuned person to enable the increased energy to flow through. This source of energy is external and limitless. It benefits the healer as well as the person receiving the treatment as it flows through the healer's energetic system first, transmuting any energetic restrictions and then travels through the system of the recipient. Attunements can sometimes have the effect of increasing the clarity of a person's perspective and this itself can bring change into an individual's life.

Another notable difference lies in its simplicity. First Degree training is taught and learned in just a couple of days. Reiki is both easy to learn and to apply. Practitioners at First Degree level are taught 12 basic hand positions or holds in which hands are usually placed on the body, although Reiki is held to be as effective above the body, within the body's energetic field, if this is preferred. An optional Second Degree level further amplifies the throughput of Reiki energy and teaches a technique of sending the energy to an absent recipient.

Whilst First Degree classes are completed in just a few days, it is recommended that at least three months elapse between First and Second Degree training in order to assimilate the energy. Both self-treatment and the treatment of others are taught at First Degree level. Students are taught to give themselves a full self-treatment on a daily basis for at least 21 days following the workshop. Some Reiki Masters suggest 30 days.

Tuition also includes exercises for developing kinaesthetic sensitivity or the sense of touch. The hands can become greatly sensitized after taking Reiki, detecting to a lesser or greater degree which areas are drawing more energy. This ability can increase with practise. Some people find they become aware of sensations such as heat emanating from their hands either during or after the attunement process or even after some time has elapsed.

The Usui System of Reiki has no belief system and there is no need to alter any beliefs that may already be held. Reiki complements other therapies and healing arts.

## Reiki Symbols

The Usui system of Reiki is based on symbols. Reiki Masters use both symbols and sacred words during attunements to create the connection between the individual and the source of life force energy. Besides the words and symbols there are also additional procedures that the Reiki Master undertakes during each initiation that complete the process of attunement.

## Self-treatment

The majority of people who decide to take Reiki First Degree training, do so because of the advantages of being able to treat themselves. As a self-treatment, Reiki is extremely simple and powerfully effective. Self-treatment can be administered anywhere at anytime, quite inconspicuously. For example, whether sitting on a train or an aircraft, the placing of hands on one's stomach to relieve a discomfort is easily done without drawing unnecessary attention to yourself. It is also said to be an excellent remedy to counter jet lag.

It is an invaluable tool for restoring depleted energy levels after a busy working day and can be used also to prevent illness developing. At the onset of a cold, a Reiki treatment can strengthen the immune system so that after a good night's sleep, the symptoms have vanished. Reiki is also effective as an emergency treatment for pain relief or to relieve anxiety before an important event.

## Treating Others

Treatment is given at a hands-on healing session that can last for over an hour. Usually the person lies down, fully clothed, facing upwards in a comfortable position on a treatment couch or any long flat surface (a bed or even a covered kitchen table will do). If it is a cool day, it may be appropriate to place a light blanket over the person receiving the treatment. It may enhance relaxation to play gentle, melodic background music. It may soothe the senses to place a few drops of essential oil of lavender in some water on a burner (or another oil as preferred) though these things are not essential.

Starting at the receiver's head, the practitioner then places their hands at a variety of positions on or above the body, each for several minutes, while working slowly down the body. The person is then asked to turn over and the back is treated.

The energy soon starts to flow and treatment is usually deeply relaxing. It is not unusual to find the person being treated has drifted into a deep sleep. Each Reiki session is different and experiences vary considerably.

*Effects of Reiki Treatment*

Reiki affects each individual in a different way. Results are determined by the needs of the person at the time of treatment. The most common elements experienced are a deep sense of peace and relaxation.

During a treatment, heat or even a cool sensation is often felt. Other responses include a fine vibration (even though the practitioner's hands are quite still throughout the treatment) or a nurturing feeling of being cocooned in a fine, gossamer wave of energy. Sometimes new ideas unexpectedly spring to mind during or following treatments. Some people might find they want to start taking up new interests such as yoga, a creative art or developing a business skill of some sort.

It is not unusual for old emotions to surface during treatment. Repressed anger or fear may be experienced. Tears may even be shed as this is released. Paula Horan in *Empowerment Through Reiki* says that Reiki has been described as a catalyst for helping to develop conscious awareness. She suggests that a symptom could be regarded as a kind of information medium to assist us to recognize and integrate aspects of our being, which we either have no conscious awareness of or have repressed. It can be this **non-consciousness**, which makes us ill. Paula Horan believes that Reiki heightens this awareness. Spontaneous emotional releases are not uncommon during treatments.

Many recipients fall asleep for the entire treatment and have no particular conscious awareness at all. Falling asleep during treatment does not affect the outcome. Reiki balances the system and healing at a subconscious level occurs. Extremely deep states of relaxation are experienced with the person feeling exceptionally refreshed, much more so than from a night's sleep. This is usually accompanied by feelings of tranquillity and well-being. Often individuals who are extremely active, find they wish to sleep more following treatment and those who lack energy find they are energetic.

Occasionally, it is possible to become aware of strong visual images during treatment and the solution to a problem may become apparent. Symptoms can diminish or disappear completely during treatment.

Occasionally slight, brief discomfort is experienced as toxins that have accumulated, are released. Convenience foods, a pressured lifestyle lacking in sleep, fresh air and relaxation can cause the body's efficient elimination system to become sluggish. The body may become accustomed to a high level of toxins accumulating and being only partially released. Reiki treatments purify the system by speeding up the elimination of the body's waste products and toxins.

It is always recommended that a large glass of water is drunk immediately after treatment and clients are advised to increase their overall intake of water or liquid, to assist this toxic release. Reiki treatments can sometimes result in additional bowel and bladder movement and even increased mucus secretion or watering of the eyes. These are further symptoms of detoxification and indicate a natural cleansing mechanism at work.

Effects of Reiki are extremely varied and totally unpredictable. This holistic treatment works on a number of levels to restore wholeness and balance. This can often happen in unexpected ways.

A more in-depth appraisal of what might be experienced giving or receiving a Reiki treatment is covered in Chapter 5.

## Treating Animals

Reiki has proven to be a very effective way of treating animals of all kinds. Practitioners who work with animals on a regular basis tell us that they have been able to cut down on their veterinarian's bills. The positive response of animals to Reiki is some proof of the astonishing effectiveness of this healing art as they are unable to respond to belief systems or psychology.

Generally, animals appear to enjoy receiving Reiki just as humans do and quickly become calm and soothed. If it is not appropriate to treat an animal hands-on, then absent healing can be used to great effect. They instinctively know how much they need and often become restless once they have drawn an adequate measure of energy. Of course, we cannot know what animals are experiencing, though usually they become quieter whilst receiving the energy and become deeply relaxed just as humans do.

General principles of treatment would be to place your hands where pain is likely to be experienced by the animal and to allow your hands to remain there for a few moments. Then gauge the response and if the animal is still relaxed, treat a few other body positions systematically.

When treating domestic animals it is a good idea initially to place your hands where the animal usually likes to be stroked. With the exception of cats, behind the ears is usually a good place to start. Cats can become restless quickly in this position. Alternatively, start by placing one hand on the head and one on the throat. Subsequently, go on to other areas on the body, just as you would a human. Very often an animal will turn and adjust its position in such a way to present the area that needs treating.

Hamsters, gerbils and other small animals are best treated by holding them in one cupped hand and placing the other hand slightly above them. Fish can be treated successfully by placing hands directly on the aquarium and allowing 15 or even 20 minutes for the energy to flow.

Horses respond well to Reiki and we have heard of horse breeders using it extensively. It has been particularly effective with accelerating relief from colic.

Family pets may exhibit indirect responses to Reiki too. Following our workshops we are often told by participants that their pets run into the room at the beginning of a Reiki treatment. They usually make themselves comfortable under the table or couch and remain there until the treatment has concluded. Pets often react in uncharacteristic ways after their owners have been attuned and take a short while to adjust to the changes perceived. Passive pets have been known to suddenly charge round and round a room and then promptly settle themselves into the lap of their owner where they remain for an unusually long time. Other pets who are usually reserved, suddenly become much friendlier and more spontaneous.

## Reiki and Plants

Much has been written about the secret life of plants and scientific tests have shown how they react to our emotions. Plant life is said to respond to love and care on an energetic level and it would be difficult to dispute the therapeutic benefit of time spent gardening. Knowing this, it would not be hard to appreciate that plants, trees and shrubs could benefit from Reiki, just as humans and animals do. It could even be said that there is even an exchange of energy as plants in a subtle way, radiate back life affirming properties.

'There are only two ways to live your life. One is as though nothing is a miracle. The other is as if everything is.'

*Albert Einstein*

# CHAPTER FOUR
# REIKI FOR PERSONAL HEALING

'I happen to believe that we make our own destiny. We have to do the best with what God gave us.'

*Mama from Forrest Gump*

## Discovering Our True Purpose

As well as being a healing art, Reiki is also a path for personal development. As human beings, we all have a basic desire to contribute positively to the world and make a difference to fellow beings, as well as to improve and enjoy life as much as it is possible to do so.

We acknowledge that each of us has a significant contribution to make and in our hearts we are aware that we each have a higher purpose, even though it may not be apparent to us at a conscious level. The stresses and strains of life often distance us from the path that could lead to the fulfilment of our true destiny and subsequently could cause inner conflict, distress and possibly ill health.

As well as enhancing physical well-being, Reiki often increases mental clarity, restores emotional balance and deepens our spiritual connection. It is not unusual to find that our intuition develops and sudden inspiration serves to alter our present perspective to such a degree, that we start to make changes in our lives. Instead of the usual conditioned response, we find there is another option and we take it. As time goes by, we take many different decisions and our lives gradually change.

It is at these times that we become more aware and more in tune with our higher purpose. The decisions and choices that we make, bring us back on course in the direction that we are intended to follow.

The adjustments might only be subtle but after some time, these alterations amount to substantial changes. It may be that working one hour less each day enables us to simplify our lives to such an extent that it is possible to be home early in time to enjoy the sunset. One day, after witnessing a marvellous spectacle of nature further inspiration to take up a new hobby might emerge, from which eventually a rewarding career is launched. The overall change might allow the individual to enjoy life more and be more closely aligned with his or her true life's purpose.

## Self-empowerment

Inner transformation can occur on a number of levels. Our experience of life can often be restricted by the limitations of our own beliefs. Our thought processes may alter completely as our self-awareness grows.

We each have a multitude of thought processes, both positive and negative and it is the results of these processes that form our experiences. Some of these are positive, enjoyable experiences and some unrewarding and negative. For example, two people might choose to visit a large city. One might believe that cities are terrible, unsafe places where cars are stolen, people are overcharged and noise levels are unacceptably high. The other might believe that cities are exciting, thrilling places to visit where it is possible to enjoy magnificent cultural attractions, sophisticated shops and stimulating people. Both would clearly have different experiences in that city even from the same vantage point; one noticing only traffic, litter and pollution and the other seeing the parks, the architecture and the creative window displays.

Negative thoughts can ultimately prevent us from achieving our full potential. Increased clarity through Reiki can help us to become aware of and even eliminate negative beliefs, releasing us to enjoy a deeper understanding of ourselves and a greatly improved inner connection with our higher selves.

This awareness can develop understanding of the relationship between negative thoughts and physical problems. Many psychotherapists find that strong emotions can be internalized within the body. Often at the point when their clients release limiting beliefs about themselves in therapy, their aches and pains spontaneously disappear. Similarly deep tissue bodyworkers such as those who practice Rolfing or Feldenkrais find that therapy releases strong emotions and it is not unusual to find treatment provoking a healing crisis as repressed feelings come to the surface. When this happens, healing has usually begun.

Reiki helps us to gently develop conscious awareness and release repressed emotion. As well as relieving physical tension and mental stress, a feeling of confidence usually begins to grow. Reiki treatment generates feelings of confidence to face changes and to make decisions from a more balanced perspective. Reiki energy balances, aligns and integrates what is going on in our systems. Each time a treatment is received, the process continues.

Clearly, healing takes place on more than just a physical level and the power of mind too is important. Reiki is a powerful tool that can help the individual release emotional blockages and move forward with confidence and clarity.

# PART TWO
# HEALING WITH REIKI

# CHAPTER FIVE
# REIKI TREATMENTS

## RECEIVING A REIKI TREATMENT

Reiki has grown tremendously in popularity over the last ten years or so and treatment is now widely available at nearly every holistic clinic or complementary medicine centre in Britain, Europe, the USA, Australia and many other countries. Short treatments or brief demonstrations of Reiki are available at most health exhibitions where a range of complementary therapies are featured. Additionally, many practitioners practise from their own homes or may be mobile and able to travel and offer Reiki to clients at a more suitable or convenient location.

As we are all individuals, reactions to treatment vary considerably. The most common element experienced is one of deep relaxation and usually a feeling of warmth in particular areas of the body. Reactions can occur both in the person receiving Reiki and the person giving the treatment as both are receiving the healing energy.

It is not uncommon to experience tingling, vibration, warmth, cool areas, twitches, crying, laughter and stomach rumblings. Sometimes it is possible to become aware of an old wound as the scar tissue receives healing. Occasionally a brief discomfort is even felt for a short while, which is usually the surfacing of some tension held in a particular area. This is unusual. It is more typical to experience a blissful, euphoric feeling that enables you to sink into a deep state of relaxation.

During a full treatment, it is usual to lie down, so it is not uncommon to fall asleep or into a 'Reiki slumber', as we have come to name it. Treatment is no less effective when the recipient has slept through it entirely. It may be just what is required.

Following treatment, many people feel rather dreamy and relaxed and may need to sit down for a while to become grounded again before driving a car.

It is recommended that at least a glass of water is drunk

following treatment as toxins are loosened during treatment that need flushing through the system. Ideally liquid intake, preferably water, should be increased considerably over the 24–48 hour period following treatment. This is for two reasons. This prevents headaches caused by the presence of any toxins remaining in the system. Secondly, the energy can make you very thirsty and it would not be helpful to become dehydrated.

It is inadvisable to drink alcohol for at least 24 hours after receiving Reiki. Alcohol could have an undesirable effect on a delicate system undergoing detoxification.

Depending upon your state of well-being, it is recommended that an initial course of three to four treatments is booked, rather than just one. The effects are cumulative and it is highly likely that several treatments will be needed to complete the healing process. For pain relief for example, one session will probably relieve the discomfort, though several will enable the energy to reach the causal level of the problem and prevent further occurrences. Discomfort may be caused by tension held in a particular body part where we have internalized something going on our in our lives. Sometimes one hears 'I can't stomach this situation'. Such a stomach disorder could be a result of internalizing a problem. Reiki may provide insight as to the cause of such a complaint. When there is insight as to the cause, the symptom may be relieved very quickly.

The energy always goes to the causal level, not necessarily to the symptom. Whilst it is highly likely the symptom will be relieved by the treatment, healing at a causal level will have undoubtedly taken place. If, for example, a person is extremely tense, it is possible that the tension has been internalized, and has subsequently manifested itself as a physical problem somewhere in the body. If the treatment releases the tension and even gives insight as to where the problem originated, it can highlight areas where the person needs to make changes to their lifestyle.

Insights as to the causes of symptoms are not uncommon during a Reiki session. One of our clients had suffered from constipation for most of her life. Over the years, she had tried many orthodox medicines, herbal remedies and a number of complementary therapies without success. Before the treatment started, we suggested that she allow herself to understand why she had this disorder. As soon as this session finished, she became anxious to share her experience. She described a scene which had unfolded in her mind during the treatment, which clarified why she had suffered so long.

As a child during the Second World War, she had been sent to stay with an aunt in the country. Even though it happened a long time ago, she was able to recall the surroundings as clearly as when she was a little girl, remembering even the dress that her Aunt was wearing. She also was able to clearly remember that the toilet was situated across a yard in the back garden. It turned out that she had been severely punished on more than one occasion for using far too much toilet paper at a time when such commodities were very scarce. As soon as she realized that the fear of punishment so long ago had caused herself to become constipated out of fear, she was greatly relieved and very pleased to have reached the root of the problem. She knew that this would never bother her again and disposed of the medicines on the way out.

For further information about the metaphysical causes of specific individual symptoms, read Louise Hay's book *Heal Your Body* (see page 152) or Baginski and Sharamon's *Reiki Universal Life Energy* (see page 150.)

Not all insights highlight the cause of a symptom. Some reveal the solution. A gentleman who came for a treatment had an insight that was to change his life. He was a family man, who had been extremely wealthy. Due to some poor business decisions, a crooked business partner and the effects of the recession, he had lost everything, including his home. He was not usually interested in complementary therapies of any sort, but as he had lapsed into a deep depression and was almost suicidal, we offered him a treatment to see if it would help at all.

Uncharacteristically, he accepted and duly arrived for his first session. His self-esteem was very low and he hardly spoke before the session. He slept deeply throughout his first treatment and told us afterwards that it was the first time had relaxed for many months. He came back for several more sessions.

During what was to be the final session, he described receiving inspiration that was to bring considerable positive change. Despite having no money, no home and no hope of receiving financial backing of any kind, he knew he must return to the industry where he had started as a young man. He had received an idea during his Reiki treatment that would enable him to supply a product to a unique outlet. He decided that he would immediately start another business although having learned many lessons from his previous enterprise, he knew it would not be easy. It was extremely difficult for him to re-establish himself and he overcame many obstacles that would have deterred others. Happily, his determination has resulted in him being able to earn a living once more and successfully provide for his family.

## Healing Crisis

Sometimes, during treatment just as progress has been made, it is possible for a healing crisis to occur. Sometimes a healing crisis brings about the return of all the original symptoms. It is comforting to know that they are not back to stay. This can be an unexpectedly traumatic experience that usually marks a turning point during treatment and indicates that repressed emotions have surfaced. It is usually after this point has passed, that healing has occured.

Such a crisis can occur because of the acceleration in the course of the illness. Deep residues of emotion can surface, which cause the crisis. Other healing crises may feature uncontrollable crying or even an unexpected skin rash emerging. These usually pass very quickly and are no cause for concern in themselves. Of course it is necessary to have healing and support during a healing crisis of any nature.

Usually powerful feelings of well-being result from a Reiki treatment and it can be extremely upsetting to experience what appears to be a setback in the form of a healing crisis. Should this happen to you, know that a catharsis of this nature does not mean that treatment is unsuccessful, it should be regarded as part of the healing process.

Reactions to treatment vary enormously and results are unpredictable. This gentle, healing energy is always drawn by the person receiving the treatment and usually at the pace that suits that individual. In a sense all healing is self-healing, the healer is just providing the right conditions for healing to occur. It is then up to the recipient. After several Reiki sessions, it is usual to feel energized, positive and pain free with the confidence and enthusiasm to make the necessary changes in your life.

The cost of a Reiki treatment is usually equivalent to the cost of a body massage in your area. To find a practitioner, see Useful Addresses on page 147 for national Reiki Associations or alternatively contact your local holistic clinic.

## SELF-HEALING

Most participants on our training courses tell us that they enrolled principally because they wish to use Reiki to treat themselves. Self-treatment is very simple and effective as a means of relaxation and stress relief. Sufferers from fatigue syndromes often experience raised energy levels after taking Reiki or indeed experiencing Reiki. Hyperactivity is usually tempered by deep relaxation after taking Reiki and emotional balance is restored. Reiki often relieves pain from acute conditions, though chronic conditions often take longer and may spark a healing crisis before symptoms diminish fully.

### 21 Day Cleanse Process

During Reiki training, it is suggested that for at least 21 days, a full self-treatment is given. There are four main reasons for this:

- Daily self-treatment is the fastest way to integrate the increased energy into an individual's system. Daily treatment allows the energy to move strongly into the physical body to bring about physiological changes. It allows the balancing and integrating of emotional, mental and spiritual bodies.

- A self-cleanse mechanism is triggered by the attunements and the system starts to detoxify. Self-treatment assists this process.

- Often before channelling Reiki to others, it is necessary to heal ourselves. Receiving the energy on a daily basis in this way, facilitates the start of our own healing.

- The individual is likely to become far more aware of the flow of energy during a concentrated period of self-treatment. Additionally, it will be easier to notice the effect on others.

There are numerous benefits to completing a 21 or 30 day self-treatment period. In that time the energy becomes well integrated into the system, detoxification is completed, self-healing has begun and sensitivity to the energy is heightened.

Most people find that they thoroughly enjoy making time for these nurturing sessions and continue them long after the recommended period has elapsed. Others find that they initially encounter some less pleasant reactions. It is not unheard of to experience mild diarrhoea or sickness following training. This is usually as a result of detoxification. Very occasionally, a rash could appear or the skin. Healing always begins within and moves outwards to the surface of the body. Such a rash would not be a cause for concern and would usually indicate that healing and cleansing is occurring.

Sometimes it happens that strong emotions begin to surface during the 21 day cleansing period. This can happen at any time, thereafter. The energy provides strength to deal with any fear or other emotions that appear and we always suggest persevering with self-treatment as they rapidly diminish. Should there be issues surfacing that are difficult to deal with on one's own, it may be helpful to arrange to see a suitable therapist who can provide the necessary support and assistance on a one-to-one basis.

## Giving Yourself a Reiki Treatment: The Twelve Positions

Below is a guideline for self-treatment, which is ideal for those who have taken Reiki First Degree training. A cassette tape is available from ourselves to accompany self-treatment, details of which can be found on page 149. Although untrained people can follow the positions, they need the training to benefit fully from self-treatment, as it is only when the attunements have been received, that the increased energy starts to flow through the person's system.

Lie down and allow yourself to become relaxed and comfortable. It is suggested when giving yourself a Reiki treatment, that you stay in each position for five minutes which means that you will spend an hour giving yourself a Reiki treatment using all twelve positions.

### First Position

With your fingers closed and the hands slightly cupped, move to the first position over the eyes. Allow the hands to remain still with a light touch whilst they are placed in the various holds.

Practise will determine a touch that is too light or too heavy. At a physical level the energy transmission in this position affects the pituitary and pineal glands as well as the eyes, sinuses, nose, teeth and jaws. At an emotional level, it helps to reduce stress. At a mental level, this position helps the processes of thought and concentration, increasing clarity and improving decision making. This is also the natural position used to treat a headache. In the Bates method of natural healing it is suggested that this position is maintained for up to an hour a day to restore the balance of one's eyesight.

This position also assists in awakening the third eye, a term which many forms of eastern medicine refer to as the part of us where mental pictures are formed and where our intuition or inspiration is drawn from. There are forms of healing that work solely towards awakening the third eye, as they feel when it is activated and awakened, it allows the person to see the God or Divine within everyone and everything, allowing a state of harmony at all levels to be experienced. The third eye is said to give inner sight where it is possible to see auras and energy.

You may feel heat in your hands and the heat may seem to turn on and then when you have been in this position for a while, the heat may diminish and appear to switch off. This is a natural regulating process and happens when the body no longer needs the energy in a particular position and so the energy stops flowing or greatly reduces.

*Second Position*

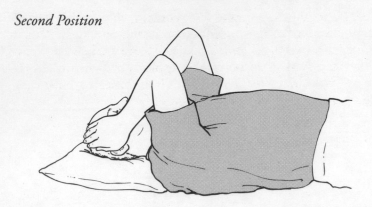

Without lifting the hands off the body, move the hands to second position over the temples. At a physical level, this position affects the brain. As the Reiki energy begins to flow into the temple areas of the head, it promotes the release of any mental tension and gradually calms the mind whilst slowing the brain's activity. It is good for headaches and seizures as well as the pituitary and pineal glands. It assists with shock and motion sickness.

At an emotional level, it works to help relieve worry, hysteria, stress and depression. This position helps to enhance dream recall. At a mental level, it assists in creating calmness, helps to improve memory retention, productivity and creativity.

Whilst in this position, the energy helps to awaken and activate the crown chakra. Chakras are an Eastern concept and refer to the various points over certain parts of the body through which energy passes. Chakras are seen as rotating wheels or spinning cones of light within the energy field or aura surrounding the body. Energy is able to pass through the chakras and enter the body. For detailed information about the function of chakras, see Chapter 6. The crown chakra is said to be the connection to cosmic information. It is the link to one's Higher Self. As the Reiki energy flows through a person in the first and second positions, it helps to integrate the right and left hemispheres of the brain. The left brain is the logical, analytical part that works with mathematics for example. The right brain is the intuitive, receptive, imaginative part. The language of the right brain is symbols.

The right and left brain also contain the feminine and masculine aspects of the body; known as yin and yang. When the energies between the two sides of the brain are balanced, it is possible for a person to be more flexible and to use whatever mode is appropriate for a situation. It is easier to effectively create situations that are desired in one's life.

*Third Position*

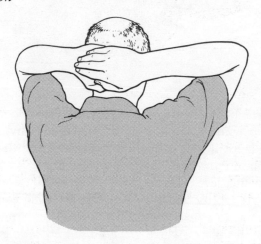

The third position with your hands at the back of your head, the base of your skull and over the occipital lobe affects weight and vision. It assists with speech and controls the nervous system for the entire body. At an emotional level, it releases stress and promotes relaxation. It relieves pain and enhances dream and past life recall. At a mental level it calms thoughts and helps relieve depression. This position is one where a mother holds a new baby before it is strong enough to hold its own head up. This is a very nurturing and supportive position for yourself (and for others).

This position affects the will centre and when this centre is constricted, one tends to give one's power away to others and not see one's own value and worthiness. This is one of the places on the body that tends to absorb a great deal of energy. There is a great need to stay balanced in this area so that maximum performance may occur.

*Fourth Position*

The fourth position over the throat and jawline at a physical level assists with strokes, tonsils, throat, larynx, thyroid, parathyroid and helps in balancing blood pressure both high and low. This position improves lymphatic drainage.

At a mental level, this position brings calmness and clarity of thought. At an emotional level it helps to bring confidence and joy as well as to relieve anger, hostility and resentment. The jaw is one of the places where we hold a tremendous amount of emotion. It is often this area where we hold on to feelings of old rage, helplessness and anger. As a culture we have a great fear of speaking our truth. We tend to swallow our words rather than speak them in anger or share them. As the Reiki energy moves into this part of the body, it begins to activate the throat. It may be felt as a pins and needles sensation or you may feel the sensation of wanting to clear your throat or cough. That's usually a good indication that there has been some holding back, that words have not been spoken.

As the energy balances this part of the body, it becomes much easier for a person to speak their truth. Every word spoken is an expression of who that person is and every time an individual does not speak their truth, it has an effect upon his or her physiological system and upon that person's life.

*Fifth Position*

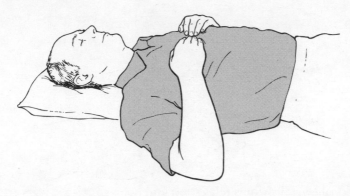

The fifth position over the heart, at a physical level treats the heart, lungs and thymus that affects the immune system and circulation. At an emotional level this facilitates the release of stress and assists in enhancing the capacity to love and be loved. At a mental level, this helps to restore balance and harmony.

As you work with yourself and others, you begin to discover that everyone has heart issues. As a culture we have learned to protect our hearts, to not allow love in or out. We have figuratively built walls of protection. As the Reiki energy moves into this part of the body, it begins to take those walls down, block by block. There are times when it is possible to feel physical movement in this part of the body.

Whilst in this position and as the blocks are being removed, it is possible to find the circulation of blood is affected allowing a greater flow throughout the body. As the energy moves into and through this area, there may be vibrations or tremors or spasms. Again, this is releasing the blocks of those walls and allowing one's heart to function in a natural state of harmony. Bringing energy into this part of the body allows one to truly experience the emotional self.

*Sixth Position*

The sixth position just below the chest, but still on the rib cage is over the solar plexus area. At a physical level, this affects the liver, stomach, spleen, gall bladder and digestion. At an

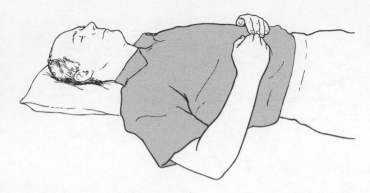

emotional level, it brings relaxation and helps to release fears and stress. At a mental level, it helps to centre oneself.

The solar plexus is our point of power in the body. It is that part that martial arts instructors teach you to draw from and to protect. When somebody hurts you, it can feel as if they have punched you in the stomach. You feel helpless, unprotected, as if you have no power. Your confidence is shattered, you doubt yourself and feel hesitant to act. When this area is in balance, one feels confident, secure and strong, moving forward with ease and putting oneself into action. There is a stream of energy that comes up from your base chakra at your tailbone, moving up through your solar plexus and you start developing greater confidence. The energy stream continues up through the heart bringing love and compassion. Simultaneously, there is a stream of energy that comes down through the top of your head, through the crown chakra bringing in wisdom through the third eye into insight. It allows you to be all that you are, in balance and in love. As the energy moves through the different parts of the body, the different chakras and the different centres it brings unity within.

*Seventh Position*

The seventh position is over the abdomen. At a physical level it affects the liver, pancreas, gall bladder and transverse colon. At an emotional level it affects issues of bitterness, fault-finding, negative feelings and frustration. This centre processes the sweets of life. Diabetes is a disease that does not allow one to properly digest sweets. The gall bladder relates to bitterness as obliquely

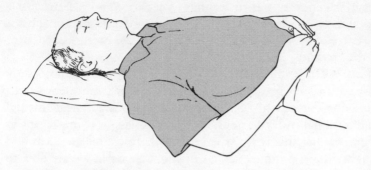

referred to in the expression 'of all the gall'. This is the centre where angry thoughts and words are held within, creating feelings of bitterness, blame and frustration.

Bringing energy to this area assists in releasing negative thoughts and gives us an opportunity to realize that we do create our lives. We create the experiences simply to learn and clearing this area provides us with the gift of learning and growing from situations and facilitates our digestion of the sweeter emotions such as harmony and joy. Treatment in this position is very calming. Using the energy, it brings balance and alignment of the physical, emotional and mental bodies, simultaneously bringing harmony at all levels.

*Eighth Position*

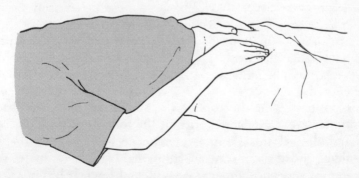

The eighth position is over the pelvic area. At a physical level, this affects lymphatic drainage and the release of toxins. It affects the large and small intestines, the bladder, issues of constipation and diarrhoea, the ovaries, uterus and prostate. At an emotional level, this centre relates to feelings of security and pleasure. At a mental level, this is the area of creativity and elimination. This is the centre of pleasure, creativity and letting go of unneeded, outdated ideas and substances.

This is the centre from which we express our sexual ecstasy and pleasure, our sexual frustration and guilt, resentment of our partner or our parent of the opposite sex. As physical, mental and emotional issues come into our awareness, it is important to remember that this is also the centre where we release ideas and thoughts that no longer serve our highest good. We are able to replace them with feelings and thoughts that can assist us to fully and joyfully express all aspects of ourselves.

*Ninth Position*

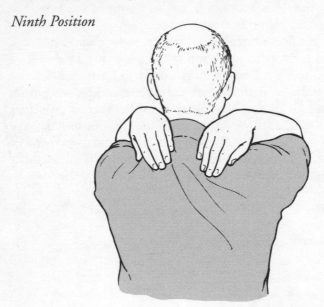

This position is at the top of the shoulders. The four back positions have a similar purpose to the four front positions. At a physical level this position affects the heart as well as the shoulders and the neck. At an emotional level, it facilitates the release of stress and burdens. At a mental level, it brings peace and harmony. This is the area where most of us experience tension, in and about our shoulders giving rise to the feelings that we're carrying the weight of the world on our shoulders.

It is possible in stressful situations to briefly place your hands on your shoulders and take a few long, slow, deep breaths. At the same time it is helpful to remind yourself to relax, whilst becoming aware of the energy as it moves in, feeling all the positive aspects of the experience as you release any tension.

*Tenth Position*

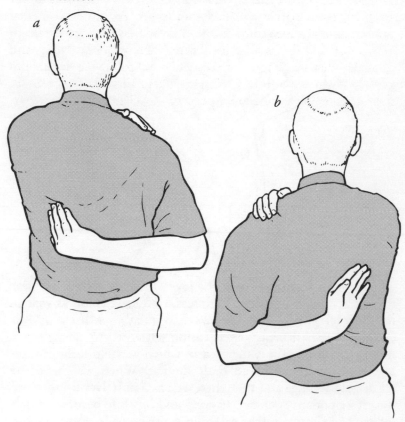

The tenth position is over the shoulder blades. This position affects the heart and the lungs at a physical level. At an emotional level it enhances the ability to love and be loved as well as facilitating the release of stress. At a mental level this position brings peace and harmony. Positions (a) and (b) show handholds to treat both sides of the shoulder blades. When spending five minutes in the other positions, allow two and a half minutes each in 10a and in 10b.

*Eleventh Position*

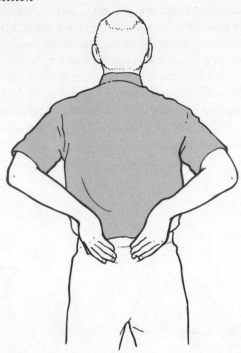

The eleventh position is over the lower back. At a physical level this affects the gall bladder, pancreas, transverse colon as well as the adrenal glands, the kidneys and the lower back. At an emotional level, it assists in releasing self-criticism, anxiety and negativity. This again is the area in which we hold feelings such as negativity, blaming and fault finding. When we choose to release old feelings and thoughts, we open ourselves up to more positive emotions such as harmony and joy. Life becomes much lighter and clearer and we experience situations in a much more positive way.

When there is a pain in the physical body, it can sometimes be recognized as a bell ringing. It may help to ask what is going on in this area. Pain may suggest there is resistance in the body, perhaps some emotion or feeling has been repressed or suppressed. When there is pain, simply begin by focusing your attention on the pain and asking 'What is my body saying to me?' or 'What is it I need to be aware of?'.

The body can be likened to a projection screen onto which our emotions and thoughts are projected. At a physical level, we tend to pay attention whereas we dismiss our thoughts and emotions all too easily. So when we have a pain in the body and we recognize that there is something out of order, it can assist us to become aware of what the cause is. Our bodies are wonderful instruments to notify us and allow us to bring disharmony into conscious awareness so that we can begin to acknowledge and deal with the real issues and causes behind the discomfort or pain.

*Twelfth Position*

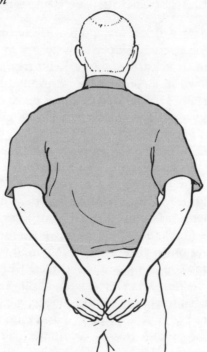

This is over the tail bone. Physically this affects the large and small intestines, bladder, uterus, ovaries, prostate and coccyx. At an emotional and mental level this is the centre of creativity and releasing. This is the seat of our power from where we create and release our desires and responses. When we hold onto old feelings or responses, we tend to concentrate on them and not make room for new ideas. Releasing old thoughts and feelings makes room for new, innovative, creative expressions. When this happens we are reaching true expressions of our potential, to become all that we can be.

Energy goes to where it is needed. Once connected to the energy, each person's evolutionary progression is encouraged. Focus is drawn to the expression of loving, positive emotions such as caring, nurturing, compassion, trusting and self accepting.

## HEALING OTHERS
## (For details of hand positions, see Chapter 10.)

A typical treatment will last for approximately one hour. In the case of children or a very weak person a twenty minute treatment is often sufficient. It is usual to give a Reiki treatment whilst the client is lying down in a comfortable position although if this is not possible for any reason, Reiki can be given sitting up in a chair or in whatever position the client is comfortable.

Giving five minutes in each position is a good guide. It is suggested that when you are working with someone else, and they have a number of severe symptoms, ideally you will want to work with them for as many as five times in the first week, four times in the next, three the next, two and then once a week for several weeks thereafter to give them optimum availability of the energy. This is in order for them to move through and balance whatever is going on in their system. If you are not able to do this, then perhaps you can give them three Reiki treatments the first week, two the next and once a week for several weeks thereafter. It is beneficial to allow a person to receive maximum exposure to the energy because the energy has a cumulative effect in the system, so the more it is used, the more it is going to bring results.

If their symptoms are more than minor, it is of course essential for them to be referred to their own medical practitioner for treatment besides receiving Reiki.

### Short Treatments
Short treatments are sometimes appropriate depending on the situation. Someone suffering from a headache can find that relief

is obtained by receiving Reiki in just two or three head positions, whilst sitting upright in a chair. In a first aid emergency, a short Reiki treatment is ideal whilst waiting for help to arrive. If a person tends to have particularly strong reactions or has powerful build-ups of energy, then again, short treatments would be preferable initially.

Short treatments may also be appropriate if someone is in considerable pain or discomfort and cannot remain still for any length of time. If a person is suffering from a particularly severe complaint, it might be wiser to avoid the problem area completely for the time being, allowing the energy to flow through from the other areas and rebalance the system in that way. Small children neither need nor appreciate lengthy treatments. Animals tend to let us know when they have had enough. When treating fewer areas for less time, it may be necessary to supplement treatment with other holistic therapies. At the very least advice on nutrition would also be beneficial.

Usui Reiki teaches twelve basic hand positions or holds that cover the major parts of the body, however there are infinitely more positions that can be used depending on the circumstances. Walter Lubeck in the book *Reiki for First Aid* describes specific positions to treat over 40 types of illness.

*Preparation*

The room in which a treatment is to be given needs to be warm as well as in a quiet location. The person receiving the treatment will usually be lying down ideally on a treatment couch, although any sufficiently long, rectangular table (such as a dining table) will suffice.

It may be helpful to cover the person with a light blanket to ensure that they do not become cool during the treatment. If the sunlight is strong, it may be preferable to draw the blinds or curtains although this is not essential. Some practitioners choose to play background music, usually with tranquil non-intrusive sounds such as music reflecting natural forest or seaside sounds, etc. Switch on an answering machine, disconnect the telephone or at least reduce its volume to prevent the person and yourself being startled during a treatment. The practitioner needs to be as comfortable as possible too and may choose to be seated for as many of the positions as possible. A chair on wheels for the practitioner may facilitate easy movement from one position to another.

If you choose to have background music playing, it may be helpful to use a cassette player with an auto-reverse function, so that the tape will turn itself over at the end of each side. An illuminated clock is invaluable to watch the time spent in each position, although it is now possible to buy various music albums especially composed for Reiki treatments with background bells indicating when to move on to the next position. (See Useful Addresses on page 147). Scented oil burners with essential oils such as lavender diluted in water may help to create a very soothing atmosphere, although care should be taken when placing these in the room to ensure they are safely positioned.

Before beginning a treatment, it is helpful to spend a few moments with the client to welcome them and to ascertain why they have come for a Reiki treatment. Explain what Reiki is, what will happen over the next hour or so, to put them at ease and give them an idea of what they may expect. Ideally the practitioner's hands should be washed before and again after the treatment. When the treatment has concluded, a full glass of water should be drunk by both the healer and the person receiving the treatment. This assists the treatment by facilitating the toxic clearout.

## Setting the Intent

Just before the treatment begins, it is a good idea to suggest that the person decides where they would like the energy to go in their lives. This only takes a moment and need not be spoken aloud. The energy may be directed to a physical pain, to enhance emotional well-being or perhaps to a particular relationship or career path. All that is necessary to do is to close the eyes and quietly say 'I would like the energy to go to . . .' and then list as many areas and situations as desired. Once the intent has been set, ensure the person knows that they can now relax and enjoy the treatment. It is not necessary to concentrate on the choice after setting the intent. Wherever it is directed, the energy will then flow. It is not unusual to find that positive and unexpected changes subsequently occur.

The practitioner briefly scans the body with their hands a few centimetres above the client at the beginning of the treatment to ascertain which areas particularly need the energy. By using the hands to sense where the energy is required, the practitioner has a guide and can focus on particular areas accordingly. It may be necessary to spend more time in one area, especially if it is a specified requirement of the person being treated.

## Recommendations for Treatment

During treatment, comfort and relaxation are paramount. It is also important to follow carefully the guidelines given in the Reiki training class. Make sure you tilt your head to one side whilst treating the head positions, so that you are not breathing over the person lying on the couch. Ensure you have not eaten excessively strong smelling or spicy foods before giving a treatment as the smell may make the person you are treating feel uncomfortable. It is also vital to position your hands carefully so that they do not come into contact with the client's nose, mouth or throat at any time. The person being treated will then be able to completely relax, without feeling their breathing is being restricted in any way.

Your hands should be relaxed and slightly arched, your fingers should be kept together and applied without pressure to the body. The treatment can be given without physical contact, a few centimetres off the body if that is preferred by either the practitioner or the person receiving the treatment. It is important to avoid hovering so lightly that it is barely felt on the body, however, as it can be uncomfortable and rather off-putting for the client. We prefer to work on the body as we feel that our society has little enough physical contact. This treatment provides a secure, non-threatening and nurturing experience for the client.

It will be natural to give Reiki to family, friends and the people closest to you when they have a need. It is a good idea to allow people to ask you for a treatment rather than simply offering it.

You may find yourself in a social situation where someone outside your immediate circle could really benefit from a Reiki treatment. Whilst it may be appropriate for you to tell them about Reiki and explain that this is something you do, it is more appropriate to let them ask you for a treatment. When a person asks, it allows them to create a vortex that Reiki can be received into. If one simply gives, very often the person doesn't really receive, because it isn't the right time for them to receive. Perhaps they aren't ready to alter their experience, because their illness or lack of finance is serving a purpose at some personal level. If they do not ask, they haven't opened to the experience, so it is preferable to allow the person to ask for Reiki.

Reiki stimulates the body's own healing mechanism but it is often helpful to support healing in additional ways in cases of chronic or extensive illness. Body purification through improved nutrition is advised to enhance the healing process.

Talking with the client before the treatment and again after the treatment is most helpful and beneficial. It is best to remain quiet during the treatment to encourage releasing and healing to occur. Sometimes a healing crisis may arise during a treatment and it is as well to be prepared for this and have a box of paper tissues in the room, in case of tears during treatment.

## The Metaphysical Meaning of Symptoms

The body is said to mirror our emotional state and sometimes stress-related symptoms can be successfully relieved, once we become aware of their cause. Events in themselves are never stressful. It is only our reaction to them that may cause us to experience stress. Often the cause is not known to us or the person on a conscious level. Experiencing a Reiki treatment can be the catalyst for increased conscious awareness. Emotional release during or after treatment is not uncommon.

An ache or a pain in itself never happens without cause. Every organ and cell in our bodies is directly or indirectly connected with all the others. If there is discomfort in one area there are probably several other areas not working sufficiently well enough to eliminate the problem. Reiki helps it to restore harmony as the whole body is treated holistically.

Sometimes the location of the discomfort can indicate the possible cause. If we are unwilling to acknowledge our feelings at a conscious level, then our body will often do this for us. An unhappy student who came for treatment was determined to assure us how happy he was with his chosen subjects. He had become too weak however to continue his studies and his parents were anxious he would not achieve the required grades for university entrance. During treatment however, it became apparent he was unhappy with his choice of coursework and had only taken them to please his parents. Once this was understood, it was decided to change his course of studies altogether and subsequently he recovered his full health.

A family man was suffering from severe shoulder pain. He had tried all kinds of treatment without success. Whilst talking about his life, it became apparent that he was 'shouldering' too much responsibility. He had literally internalized these feelings which had surfaced as shoulder pain. Following the Reiki treatment, he decided to make major changes in his life to enable him to delegate his heavy workload and enjoy some of his other interests.

Sometimes, the causes of ill-health are more obvious: poor diet, lack of exercise, too much alcohol, smoking and lack of sleep all need to be addressed before the body can function efficiently.

## When Not to Use Reiki

Reiki should not be given after a pre-operative anaesthetic has been administered or during an operation. Reiki increases awareness and it would not be helpful in this instance. However, Reiki is excellent when used to speed up the healing process after surgery. Reiki creates a balance and harmony in each person's system by reducing toxic residues which in these instances would not be appropriate or desirable. It is preferable to give Reiki before or after a chemotherapy course, rather than during treatment for this reason. Reiki is effective when a person is undergoing radiotherapy.

A brief treatment for 5–10 minutes will be beneficial to anyone (with the exception of anaesthetised pre-operative situations) but individuals taking anti-coagulants or cardiac stimulants should not receive longer than this on a regular basis. This also applies to persons prone to epileptic seizures who are taking medication for this condition. The only exception to this is just before or just after a seizure.

Should there be any reason to assume that an individual has a serious mental or physical disorder of any kind, which you are not qualified to deal with, then refer the client without delay to a suitably qualified person. If a client is taking medication and you are unsure whether Reiki will complement their treatment, ask their medical practitioner or alternatively advise the person concerned to ask their doctor whether it would be appropriate.

Reiki can be very helpful in overcoming alcohol or drug addiction as it promotes deeper levels of awareness. It is always inadvisable to treat a client who is in an inebriated condition. It is also important to advise clients to drink more water before and after treatment and especially to avoid alcohol for at least 48 hours following treatment.

As previously mentioned, it is preferable to give Reiki only when asked, except in the case of your closest family whom you may perceive to have a need for the energy, and do not wish to 'trouble you'.

Some Reiki Masters recommend that Reiki should not be given to a person wearing a pacemaker or other such aids. It would be wise to err on the side of caution and if first aid is to be given to a person with such a device, to only treat areas as far away as possible from it.

For the most part, with the exception of the above, there are few instances in which it would not be appropriate to give Reiki. Trust your instincts and if it feels right to give a treatment, then it is likely to be beneficial.

## GROUP TREATMENTS

Reiki works well as a group treatment. It is possible for two, three, four or even five people to take part in a group session. The energy is amplified with more people channelling the energy and it is very enjoyable for the person receiving the treatment. After Reiki First Degree training, all initiates are invited to an Energy Exchange. These group sessions are an ideal time to get together for an enjoyable healing evening and are far less formal than a one-to-one session.

Each person takes turns to receive and give the energy and all are grouped around the table. One person lies on the treatment couch and the others take turns to move around the different positions. The person who sits behind the head usually watches the clock, if there is not a timed music cassette playing. Each person remains in one position for three or five minutes and then moves to the next position until the group has completed that individual's treatment and it is then the turn of the next member of the group to be treated and so on, until all have given and received in this manner.

This is an excellent way for a novice healer to develop kinaesthetic ability and gain experience in a group setting. The response is usually lively and helpful to all. It is a good opportunity to share experiences and ask any questions that arise.

*Energy Circle*

An Energy Exchange usually begins with an Energy Circle. This allows the group to form an energetic circuit or link by joining hands for a moment or two and allowing the energy to flow around the circle. The Energy Circle exercise can be successfully extended into a meditation as well.

*Group Meditation*

During this session a group meditation is usually shared and distant healing is sent to people and situations. Group healing sent to war-torn situations or to friends in hospital is usually very much more powerful than that sent individually. Any excess of energy is then sent to heal the earth.

## Distant Healing

Distant healing can be sent powerfully using the method taught at Reiki Second Degree level. Usually a list of where and to whom the energy is to be sent is compiled by the group at the start of the evening. Before the group distant healing session, one member may read the list out aloud. The group sitting in a circle is then asked to visualize a ball of healing energy in the centre. Those not using the Reiki Second Degree method of distant healing could imagine their hands positioned over the ball of energy channelling more energy into the centre of the ball which then grows larger and larger until it is sent out to benefit all the people and situations throughout the world on the list previously read out.

Often Reiki sharing groups will contact the Mary McFayden Reiki Outreach Organization hotline before an Energy Exchange to find out the current world situations that Reiki groups all over the world are sending energy to (see Useful Addresses on page 147). As each sharing group collectively sends energy to world situations, the energy becomes amplified. The healing that results directly affects us all. There are numerous possibilities for sending Reiki energy to diseases or environmental crises that can have a beneficial positive effect on people and help to bring desperately needed balance and harmony to many parts of the world.

'Miracles happen every day. Now some people don't think so. But they do.'

*Forrest Gump*

# CHAPTER SIX
# COMBINING REIKI WITH OTHER METHODS OF HEALING

Reiki combines well with other complementary therapies, and indeed with conventional forms of medicine as described by Nancy Eos MD in her book *Reiki and Medicine*. Many doctors, psychologists and natural health practitioners who combine Reiki with other forms of treatment have achieved good results The possibilities for combining the various techniques are endless. Increasingly more doctors, healing practitioners, masseurs, physical therapists and psychologists participate in Reiki training workshops.

## Reiki and Hypnotherapy

Reiki combines well with hypnotherapy. Provided that the full consultation had been conducted previously, the client could benefit from hypnotherapy whilst receiving a Reiki treatment. A helpful book *Hypnotherapy and the Radiance Technique* by Van Auk gives an interesting insight into one therapist's personal experience of combining healing with hypnotherapy. From the hypnotherapist's point of view, the client would be so relaxed, there would be no need for a formal induction. The person would most likely be much more at ease and receptive to therapy and would, of course, benefit from receiving the energy at the same time.

One method we used was to begin giving hypnotherapy upon reaching position five, the heart position. We also found it was particularly effective when we coincided carefully chosen wording with the area that was being treated. Another equally effective method involves focusing on giving energy to the area or chakra point directly relating to the nature of the client's problem and using hypnotherapy whilst the energy was focused on the particular position. An excellent book describing the function of the energy chakras is *The Chakra Handbook* by Shalila Sharamon and Bodo J. Baginski.

Hypnotherapy can be used in conjunction with self-treatment by either recording or listening to a specially prepared cassette whilst receiving the energy. This can be powerfully effective. There are books available on self hypnosis that can be helpful in preparing such a tape. This would also have the benefit of being personalized to your own requirements. (See Further Reading page 152). Some examples of using visualizations during self-treatment for losing weight, stopping smoking and gaining confidence are given in Chapter 7.

For those clients not open to receiving a Reiki treatment, Reiki can be sent during a hypnotherapy session to assist during a healing crisis or to generally assist the client to move beyond a painful episode with inner strength and clarity.

## Reiki and Aromatherapy, Reflexology, Shiatsu, Massage and Other Bodywork

Those who practise reflexology, massage, aromatherapy, shiatsu and other forms of bodywork find that their work is enhanced by combining it with Reiki. Usually this is very satisfying and effective for the client.

Whether or not Reiki is used formally in conjunction with a particular type of bodywork, the healing energy is transmitted whenever a treatment is given. One massage therapist did not tell her clients she was taking Reiki and did not use it in combination. The energy flowed through anyway during the bodywork. The following week a particularly sensitive lady who came for a regular massage, observed that the treatment that day somehow felt special although the therapist had not done anything different, and asked why this should be.

Some therapists prefer to keep treatments separate and offer perhaps a Reiki treatment one week and their particular bodywork the next. Others prefer to use it in combination and the variations are numerous.

Additionally aromatherapy and other massage oils can be charged with Reiki by holding the container in cupped hands and treating with Reiki for a few moments before the massage. The effectiveness and potency of the ingredients are enhanced.

The energy passes easily through glass and plastic as well as through plaster casts and of course clothes.

Burning essential oils (usually a few drops of the essential oil diluted into water) whilst giving a Reiki treatment is powerfully therapeutic. Recommended oils include lavender, which promotes relaxation. Clary sage is known to be a powerful stimulant to awaken the third eye. Sandalwood has a nurturing quality and would encourage a conducive atmosphere for releasing any fears. Lemon verbena assists in the releasing of old ideas and patterns of behaviour. There are many books and indeed articles in magazines now available on the characteristics of essential oils and the inclusion of one or two would undoubtedly enhance any healing environment.

## Reiki and Meditation

Whilst being attuned, participants in Reiki workshops find that they naturally slip into a meditative state, even if they have never meditated before. Those who do meditate on a regular basis find that their meditation deepens considerably after being attuned and they are able to achieve a deeper state for longer periods much more effortlessly. See Chapter 9 for further details on meditation.

## Reiki and Allopathic Medicine

Reiki also combines well with conventional medicine. Doctors who have taken Reiki training can use Reiki to diminish pain whilst in the process of setting bones or to speed up healing of post-operative scars. Emergency room doctors can use Reiki to reduce pain and swellings or to reduce anxiety whilst the patients are being treated.

Paediatricians find it helpful in the treatment of young patients. New-born infants in intensive care benefit from Reiki treatment. Many nurses are drawn to Reiki and can use it effectively to soothe patient's suffering, relieve pain and accelerate the healing process. Doctors who have taken Second Degree Reiki have sent their patients distant healing during consultations which has subsequently assisted the healing process.

Reiki can also reduce the toxic effect of medicines and drugs. The side effects are minimized. Additionally using Reiki may mean that less medication is required for pain relief in a post-operative situation. The possibilities are endless.

## Reiki and Homeopathy

Reiki works well in conjunction with homeopathic treatments and will strengthen their action which may result in reduced length of treatment.

## Reiki and Flower Remedies

Flower remedies are the life force essence of flowers. They are a vibrational medicine and work in a similar way to homeopathic remedies. New physics as well as ancient sages tell us that matter and energy are two very different forms of the same energy that everything in the universe is composed of. These fields of energy have motion and vibrate at different rates. The slower the vibratory rate, the denser the matter, such as rocks, trees or bones etc. The faster the vibrational rate, the more subtle the energy, such as light, sound or colour etc. Very high frequency energy is able to bring about changes in energy patterns and this is what is known as vibrational medicine. Such remedies help to activate the body's own self-healing mechanism by raising the vibrational level of energy patterns. Flower remedies work well in conjunction with Reiki restoring balance by raising the vibrational level of the person.

## Reiki and the Chakras

Many forms of eastern medicine recognize the existence of a number of energy points known as chakras in different locations over the body. They have been described as energy centres and there are seven main chakra points. Clairvoyants see chakras as rotating wheels or as spiralling discs of light. Each chakra is said to vibrate at a different rate through being charged by the energy of the sun entering each chakra in the form of light. This causes each chakra to resonate with a particular vibrational frequency each of which corresponds to a different sound and colour. Certain music and colour improves the functioning of each chakra in this way. Crystals, flower essences and homeopathic medicines each have vibrational frequencies that the chakras respond to, which evokes a healing response by means of sympathetic resonance.

The etheric body which envelops the physical body absorbs fine levels of energy and information from the environment through the chakra points to the physical body. The positions of the chakra points correspond to the endocrine glands in the physical body. The endocrine system controls the hormone balance within a person. The hormones have a powerful effect on the moods and emotion of the individual. If the chakras are out of balance, then it often happens that the endocrine system is also out of sorts and the person concerned may be suffering as a result.

*The seven major chakra positions*

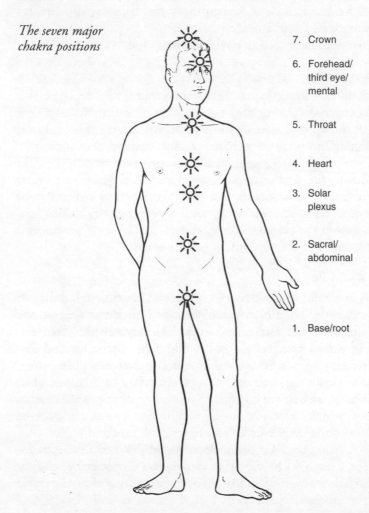

7. Crown

6. Forehead/ third eye/ mental

5. Throat

4. Heart

3. Solar plexus

2. Sacral/ abdominal

1. Base/root

It is no coincidence that the Reiki hand positions are also over the main chakra points. Sometimes, it may happen that one particular chakra is working less well than the others. When this happens, all the chakras fall out of balance. It is far better to treat all the chakras to restore balance throughout the body. This is why a full Reiki treatment is always preferable to shorter sessions.

As a human being matures, the chakras also develop and mature. If a person's development is inhibited for any reason, their functioning may be reduced which could affect a person's state of health. Reiki energy improves and balances the chakras enhancing well-being at all levels.

The seven major chakra positions are as follows:

### The Base Chakra

This is in the lower pelvic area and governs the reproductive area, the spinal column and the kidneys. It is in this area that our will for survival is at its most powerful. Unless this chakra is functioning properly, a person cannot develop harmoniously. Blockages in this area may result in mental symptoms, rigid attitudes to life and extreme opinions. On a physical level, a malfunctioning base chakra can result in physical symptoms of the bones, teeth and spine as well degenerative illnesses and complaints of the large intestine, the ovaries, bladder, uterus and the prostate. The corresponding colour is red.

### The Sacral Chakra

This is in the lower abdominal region and governs our ability to perceive the world and interact with it. This is the area of our self-perception and our sexual area. Blockages in this area can result in fear of physical closeness, frigidity, impotence and diseases relating to our body fluids or the organs processing these fluids, such as the kidneys, lymph glands and bladder. The colour for this chakra is orange.

### The Solar Plexus Chakra

This is situated between the abdomen and the breast bone and is the area from which we draw our personal power. The solar plexus chakra governs the left side of the brain and is associated with the intellect. It is linked to the pancreas, gall bladder and digestive processes. Blockages result in mental symptoms, changes in personal status and false claims to power. Physical symptoms include stomach and pancreatic complaints as well as digestive disorders. Disorders can produce excessively dominant behaviour. The colour for this chakra is yellow.

### The Heart Chakra

This is over the heart and is our emotional centre. This area governs our relationship issues and if balanced allows us to accept the world and other people as they are. It is also the area of self love. Blockages in this area result in mental symptoms such as inflexibility and often manipulation in relationships with others with a reduced capacity to give and receive love. Physical symptoms frequently result in conditions such as heart complaints and malfunctioning of the thymus gland as well as circulatory disorders, lung diseases, cramps and spasms. Emotional blockages can result in depression or particularly self-sacrificing behaviour. The colour for this chakra is green.

### The Throat Chakra

This chakra is situated over the throat and governs the area of self-expression. This area also regulates metabolism and is associated with communication. Blockages can result in extremely dominant behaviour. Chakra imbalance in this area can sometimes be diagnosed through irregular voice pitch and tones. Physical symptoms can include general disturbances to growth and development and disorders of the tonsils and throat as well. There is a connection between the throat and the solar plexus chakras. Imbalance of this chakra can result in tendencies to exert excessive power over others. The colour for this chakra is turquoise blue.

### The Third Eye Chakra

This is situated in the centre of the forehead and governs our intuition. On a physical level this chakra affects the pituitary and pineal glands which influence growth. This area corresponds to the creative right side of the brain and is associated with our inner vision. People whose third eye chakra functions particularly well often develop clairvoyance. Blockages can result in headaches, visual problems, hyperactivity and conversely sluggishness.

Hyperactivity of this chakra can result in excessive mental activity. This can lead to a multitude of 'visions'. These 'visions' can often be of an alarming and possibly threatening nature. This may also be accompanied by increased fear and reduced clarity.

Under-functioning of this chakra may cause disinterest in the world, aimlessness, lack of personal vision with a tendency to feel disconnected. The colour for this chakra is indigo.

### The Crown Chakra

This chakra is situated on the top of the head and is linked to the pineal gland. This is our spiritual centre and from here we develop and interpret our understanding of love, beauty, art, religion, our connection to all living things and to the divine. Blockages can result in feelings of isolation, seclusion and despair. A crown chakra that is functioning well enables the individual to develop a greater understanding as to the nature of the divine. The colour for this chakra is purple.

### Chakra Balancing

To assess the condition of the chakra system, it is possible to use your hands to try to sense where the movement has slowed down. Alternatively a clairvoyant may simply see whether the wheels of light are spinning appropriately. Should there not be enough time for a full Reiki treatment, the chakras can be balanced by giving a short session.

### Using Reiki to Balance the Chakras

Sitting in a chair, place one hand on the forehead and one on the back of the neck. Then place both hands on the shoulders. After this, place one hand on the chest and one on the back. Next, place one hand on the solar plexus and one hand on the corresponding position on the back. Finally place one hand on the abdomen and one hand on the tailbone. This short treatment will balance the chakras effectively.

### Meditation to Charge Chakras

Make yourself comfortable sitting upright on a chair and take two or three deep breaths.

Allow your breath to become regular and as you breathe in again, breathe in the colour red. See your entire body fill with the colour red. Slowly bring your awareness to your pelvic region. Visualize a spiral of red light spinning (looking directly at the chakra from outside the body) under your body in the pelvic region.

When this spiral of red light is spinning vigorously, visualize yourself breathing in orange, filling yourself with orange light. See a spiral of orange light spinning in the abdomen region.

Following this, feel yourself breathing in yellow. Visualize your entire being filling with yellow light as you breathe in and out. Bring your attention to the solar plexus region. See a spiral of yellow light spinning in the solar plexus region.

Next, allow yourself to breathe in green. With each breath in, breathe in more green light. Focus on your heart chakra and visualize a green spiral spinning powerfully with every breath that you take.

And now see yourself breathing in blue. Feel yourself filling up with blue light. Focus on your throat area and visualize a blue spinning spiral rotating in your throat area as you breathe in the blue light.

Next breathe in indigo, the combined colour of blue and violet. Visualize this colour filling your body as you breathe in and out. Focus on your third eye area, feel the indigo spinning spiral moving into the third eye with every breath.

Next, breathe in violet. See your whole body filling up with violet light. Concentrate your focus on your crown area on the top of your head. See a spiral of violet light spinning in this area. Feel it with every breath taken in.

Now, breathe in pure white light. Fill yourself with bright white light. See the spiral of white light begin to spin powerfully on to and around the top of your head spreading throughout your entire body. See this column of brilliant white light cascading down purifying, invigorating and energizing your whole system that is now connected to this vast column of white light which stretches up to infinity.

When you are ready, and your chakras are sufficiently charged, slowly open your eyes.

## Clearing Energy Blockages

Energy flows freely through the body when we are in optimum health physically, emotionally and mentally. When we feel threatened or view the world as an unsafe place, we create energy blocks, reducing the flow of energy through our systems. We create blockages as an energetic defence system.

Occasionally whilst giving treatments, certain areas may seem to draw very little energy compared to the surrounding areas and may even feel cool to the touch. You may intuitively sense that such an energy block is present. Reiki energy is very powerful and will gently break down such blocks, given time. However to speed the breakdown of such a blockage, visualize yourself grasping the stuck energy and pulling it up and out of the system. See yourself sever its connection to the body with your hand and either project a laser beam from your third eye area to dissipate it or hand it on to angels or beings of light who remove it. This exercise will free the area concerned and you may well find that area now accepting more Reiki energy than previously. For more information on types of energy blocks and dispersing them, read *Hands of Light* by Barbara Brennan

## Sound and Reiki

Sound has a powerful therapeutic effect. Humming and singing has always profoundly affected mood and well-being and it may be that sound holds a particular vibrational frequency that has the potential to be used far more extensively than at present.

Musician Steve Halpern amongst others, composes music relating to specific sound frequencies in order to stimulate healing. His compositions have been played in numerous clinics and hospitals achieving successful responses from a great many people. The resonance of this music is said to tune the chakra system and enhance well-being. Tribal people have always used singing and chanting to connect with their environment, entertain, lift their spirits and heal their sick.

There are currently voice and sound workshops available that teach various types of singing and chanting. Teachers such as Jill Purce and Chris James have enabled many people to re-connect with the power of their own voice and use it for healing and enjoyment. Techniques taught include toning, Mongolian overtone chanting and various other group chanting techniques. The singing that these groups are guided to produce in such workshops is astonishingly beautiful and never fails to surprise and delight the participants. Chanting and singing is a very powerful medium for healing and there are books available which define various techniques for using sound to heal particular parts of the body or particular disorders.

Only recently a resonance was said to have been discovered by Western scientists that apparently evoked a powerful healing response. This resonance was apparently identical to that emitted by the gong which has been used for healing by traditional cultures for centuries.

Music is often played in the background whilst a Reiki treatment is being given to enhance healing and promote a relaxing environment. Almost any tranquil music is appropriate for healing. On page 148 there is a list, including some favourite recommendations of ours, plus a number of musical albums specially composed for Reiki treatments. There is also a list of mail order suppliers of music for relaxation on page 148.

## Colour and Reiki

All the colours of the rainbow are used in healing and each one has its own effect. There are many books available on colour's powerful healing effects. Theo Gimbel has written several books on the subject. Each one of us uses colour therapy when we select a particular colour to wear each day. Hospitals have been known to use particular colours on their walls to speed up healing responses. Prisons have experimented with particular colours to reduce aggression. Each colour has been known to elicit a particular healing response. When a particular colour is absent from the auric field of the individual, ill health often results. A specially trained therapist may determine which colour would most benefit an individual's auric field and the person could then be treated by possibly being enveloped in colour rays from a specially designed lamp.

Alternatively, a healer may visualize a particular colour being beamed to a person during a treatment. Sometimes it is helpful to advise a client to wear a particular colour that is appropriate to the chakra colour where emotional release is necessary. Underactive chakras can be restored by being stimulated with the appropriate colour.

There is always a long line of people waiting at Mind Body & Spirit type exhibitions to have a photograph of their aura taken and then interpreted. At one such exhibition, an exhibitor was displaying photographs of a person's aura before and after a Reiki treatment. There was a multitude of colours in the auric field following the treatment.

The colours of an individual's aura change not just from day to day but from moment to moment. However if an aura is greatly depleted, external assistance such as healing or colour therapy may be needed to replenish the energy field. Skilled interpreters and healers with a clairvoyant ability claim to be able to diagnose illness in the auric field before it manifests in the physical body.

Visualization can be used to cleanse, balance and replenish the auric field using the colours of the rainbow. This exercise can be used in the shower or simply as a meditation to relax and restore you at any time, in which case a waterfall may be substituted as a more appropriate setting.

*Taking a Colour Shower*

Imagine that as you take a shower, the water has a magical quality being able to radiate each of the brilliant colours of the rainbow.

As you switch on the shower and step into it, visualize the vibrant red colour of the water warming and energizing you. As this colour pours down on you, take a moment to feel yourself infused with the beautiful, vibrant red colour, releasing all your fears.

After a moment, see the water become a brilliant shade of orange. Orange opens you to experience joy and allows you to release shame and guilt. Orange relieves cramp and strengthens bronchial tubes. Feel the orange colour around you.

And now the water becomes a bright shade of yellow. Feel the yellow water cleanse emotional pain and stimulate the lymphatic system. Yellow clears the mind and invigorates the digestion system.

Visualize the water becoming a brilliant shade of green balancing and restoring the physical body and stimulating the pituitary gland. Green purifies the whole system renewing your expression of love and forgiveness.

See the water change to a beautiful, cooling, magical blue. Blue enhances self-expression allowing you to speak your truth. Feel the blue all around you, allowing you to express yourself according to your true self.

The water changes to indigo and purple. Visualize yourself surrounded by indigo and purple, stimulating your own healing power and wisdom. Indigo stimulates the third eye awakening your intuition, and purple increases your cosmic connection. Feel the calming influence of the velvet dark colours of indigo and purple.

Finally visualize the water becoming brilliant white light. White takes away any pain and shows you the peace and joy within your own spirit. Take a moment to enjoy the white light surrounding you, filling you with peace and harmony before finishing your rainbow shower.

## Crystals and Reiki

There is a powerful resonance that exists between living beings and crystals and many ways in which crystals can be used with Reiki to promote healing. Crystals are said to amplify and focus energy that can be directed at specific energy blockages in order to repair disruptive patterns in the etheric field, sometimes even before a physical illness has manifested. They cannot however remove the negative thought patterns that may have contributed to causing the illness in the first place. This is where Reiki comes in and goes directly to the causal level. Crystals can work well in conjunction with Reiki.

### Quartz Crystals for Energy Blocks

Quartz crystals are especially effective for powerfully directing healing energy and breaking down blockages. They are a helpful supplement to Reiki healing being ideal for programming with healing thought forms. They can treat specific organs and disorders as well as having a calming effect on people who normally find it difficult to relax.

Quartz crystals can be used as a way of removing an energy block during a Reiki treatment. It is best to use a long crystal for this purpose and when an area appears to be drawing very little or no energy, point the crystal at the block and move it rapidly in a clockwise direction, up and away to free up the blockage. This area may then receive more energy.

Quartz can be used in a similar manner to repair damaged chakras or energize scar tissue. Crystals can be placed in a particular position on the person receiving a Reiki treatment to further help a particular organ or to generally complement the energy.

Quartz crystals radiate much beauty and light and can be carried easily in the pocket to heighten positive interaction with others on a daily basis. In a working environment where there is a certain amount of ongoing conflict, it is often recommended that quartz crystals are regularly cleansed and re-programmed for effective results.

## *Amethyst Crystals and Intuitive Development*

Amethyst reflects the purple ray which is one of the colours for the third eye centre and symbolizes change of consciousness and altered awareness. It is therefore most effective for stimulating the awakening of the third eye and intuitive abilities. It helps to raise general awareness and encourages development of the self. Amethyst also brings clarity to allow us to recognize our own individual path and conveys vitality so that we are able to follow it. Amethyst is ideal to use when meditating. It can also be placed directly on the third eye to stimulate it and can usher in a tranquil state of inner calm. It works well in conjunction with rose quartz that soothes and opens the heart to bring about a peaceful balance of mental and emotional energies.

## *Rose Quartz for Healing Trauma*

Rose quartz opens the heart as its warm, pink vibration corresponds directly to the heart chakra. Rose quartz is said to heal trauma and release deep blockages as well as feelings of anxiety. The properties of this crystal allow you to open to self love and the love of others. It heals deep wounds and opens the heart to love. It is a stone for those who have never before been able to experience the joy of living. Often when children are brought up without the love and nurturing they need, they are unable to love themselves and subsequently unable to love others. Unless deep inner healing takes place, that person is trapped in a vicious circle unable to provide love for their own children. Rose quartz allows healing to take place by penetrating the inner chamber of the heart chakra and dissolving the emotional burdens trapped within. Rose quartz would be an ideal complement to Reiki when healing heart issues as the stone could be carried on the person whilst healing continues.

*Moonstone for Balancing the Emotions*

Moonstone helps to soothe and balance the emotions and acts as a guardian at the gateway to the subconscious. This allows a greater awareness to unfold. Moonstone is very good for balancing the masculine and feminine aspects of ourselves. It helps men to become more in tune with the feminine aspect of themselves and allows women greater emotional and hormonal balance during their menstrual cycle. Moonstones help to neutralize negative emotions allowing calmness and peace of mind to prevail.

Many books and courses are now available on the subject of crystals and there are numerous possibilities for combining Reiki with many different types of crystals for healing and transformation.

## Reiki, Imagery and Healing

Images are common in Reiki and can sometimes offer clues as to the origin of an illness. Imagery is a powerful medium and it is sometimes possible to use the imagery received in a creative way to elicit a healing response. By reversing or altering the images received, a healing response may be stimulated. This is a particularly effective technique to use with children.

One child who had a bed-wetting problem received an image of a hose pipe that was out of control. When she was asked to visualize a tap being put in to control the water and subsequently turn it off, the bed wetting stopped. Such visualization can stimulate a powerful healing response as it is a very effective way for the mind to communicate with the body. An appropriately chosen image can produce very successful results in different situations.

Many extraordinary examples of healing using imagery have been described by Bernie S. Siegel, *Love, Medicine & Miracles*, who has adapted a number of such techniques and incorporates these in his work as a doctor and surgeon. The difficulty is often in determining the most appropriate image and this can only be done by the person who is unwell. It would be difficult to compile an ideal list of visualizations for particular illnesses as the image would need to mean something personally to that person. Books have been written with suggested imagery to use to stimulate a healing response and these could be personalized and adapted for individual use (see Further Reading on page 152). The Silva Mind Control course has successfully used imagery to evoke powerful healing responses and many other results.

When Reiki is being sent to heal a specific problem, it would be helpful to ask the client to carefully observe any images that come to mind in connection with the illness. Very often people who have inflammation in a particular area visualize a fire. It may be worth asking them to visualize putting out the fire and to take steps to ensure the fire could never start again. It is more effective if the individual is able to use self-created imagery. Reiki can work well in conjunction with imagery and can inspire the individual to take an active part in their own healing process.

# CHAPTER SEVEN
# OTHER WAYS OF USING REIKI

'If you knew who walks beside you at all times on this path that you have chosen, you would never experience fear again.'

*A Course in Miracles*

## Asking for Unseen Help

Mystical thinkers and sages have always told us that we live in an interactive universe. We did not always believe this to be the case. Some years ago, long before we had discovered Reiki, our own lives seemed to be filled with pain and struggle at one particular point. One evening, we came across a chapter in a book that focused on the possibility of other intelligent beings co-existing alongside ourselves on other dimensions. We remember asking the universe for help out aloud that night and subsequently forgetting all about it.

We had recently been bereaved of both Chris's parents within a short space of time. It was not long after this that we found ourselves sitting in a crowded spiritualist church for the first and only time in our lives. Whilst sitting there hearing messages being delivered to several other people, the medium suddenly turned to address us. Despite any good intentions, scepticism would not have allowed us to have drawn comfort from vague 'messages' that could have applied to numerous people. Besides, the relationship we had enjoyed with Chris's mother was an uneasy one, to say the least.

One of the first things the medium said was 'They know you have asked for help and help is there from many sources'. Our faces must have registered absolute astonishment as she then went on to identify Chris's mother and describe her character and physical appearance. The medium cannot have begun to imagine our incredulousness when she subsequently delivered a very warm and quite unexpected apology for the way in which our relationship had been conducted. Those few moments were transformational.

Although we were never again to return to the spiritualist church, the prospect of having received a response from unseen dimensions was extremely exciting. We spent all our spare time over the following months reading all we could on the nature of metaphysics. We attended lectures, enrolled on courses and generally learned as much as possible about the esoteric nature of the universe. We learned to ask for answers and opportunities. Each time, the universe responded. Sometimes the answer came to mind unexpectedly. Sometimes the answer would 'coincidentally' be included in a magazine article in a waiting room or we would be seated next to someone on a train who was just the person to help.

We also realized that you have to ask clearly for what you want. When we were later to learn Reiki, the teacher emphasized the importance of this. Be careful you don't ask for struggle. If you would like to meet a new partner, be specific. One student who had split up from her partner was disappointed that her relationship hadn't worked out. She told us that she had asked the universe for a pleasant, kind partner and for some reason it hadn't worked out. I asked her why she was unhappy and it turned out her partner was pleasant enough but his company wasn't as stimulating as she would have preferred. She subsequently made a far more detailed list of characteristics she would like her future partner to have and enlisted the universe's help. It is important to ask for what you want specifically and leave the delivery details to the universe.

One woman missed a job interview because of a rail delay and decided to take an earlier train home. On this train she was to meet her future partner whom she later married. They subsequently lived by the sea in a warmer climate, which was exactly what she had originally desired.

Whilst it is perfectly acceptable to ask for whatever you would like for yourself, it wouldn't be appropriate to ask on anyone else's behalf. That would be interfering. It may be tempting to ask if someone could win the lottery next Tuesday as they have money worries, but it simply may not be in the best interests of that person to suddenly find themselves extremely wealthy. On the contrary, it may create a whole new set of problems for them. The Beatles were not far wrong when they sang 'Money can't buy me love' and could have added that 'Money can't buy me happiness either'.

At some level, people may be learning from their lack of abundance and need to work it out for themselves. Somebody once said that it was far better to teach a man to fish than to provide a great meal of fish en croute and we have to agree with that. If we can show someone how they might fix their own problems and then let them get on with it, it is a far better long term solution.

Every time you give yourself a Reiki treatment, it is possible to ask for whatever you want and to send the Reiki energy to the areas in your life where it is most needed. Be sure to be aware and keep a look out for the delivery.

## Reiki and Pregnancy

Women who are having a baby enjoy Reiki as it helps to alleviate many of the usual symptoms associated with pregnancy, such as morning sickness and lower back pain. The baby also seems to enjoy the energy and there is often a lively kick in response to the flow of energy. A daily Reiki treatment (or a weekly treatment if this is not possible) especially on the abdominal area, the heart, the solar plexus and the temple will help the body to handle the changes and the increased demands that pregnancy puts upon it.

After the birth, Reiki can be used effectively to help the baby recover quickly from the trauma of being born and can also help with any complication that may arise. The energy will be flowing whenever the mother is stroking the child and this will be very soothing and comforting for the baby.

Reiki has been known to assist the fertility process. It has also been known to help when a pregnancy ran into difficulties, in addition to a doctor's treatment, and the baby was later born, safe and healthy.

## Reiki and Children

'I have many flowers' he said 'but the children are the most beautiful flowers of all.'

*The Selfish Giant* by Oscar Wilde

## Children Learning Reiki

As a family, we regularly enjoy Energy Exchanges. It is a special time. Before our eight-year-old son was attuned to receive Reiki for himself, he often placed his small hands on the feet of his sisters and joined in with the rest of the family.

One day he asked whether he was really channelling the energy along with the rest of the family. We told him truthfully that he wasn't. From that point, he asked nearly every day to be 'tuned' as he called it. Eventually we asked him why he wished to be 'tuned' and he replied that he wanted to be able to give Reiki to his pet hamster or heal his cuts in the playground.

He was too young to join in a workshop so we decided to attune him each evening for four nights instead of his bedtime story. It was incredible to see how pragmatic he was. He experienced the attunements as brilliant lights and accepted this with simplicity and some wonder too. Since that time he has really participated in Energy Exchanges and his little hands become red hot. Young children can only channel the energy for a short period of time and our son is no different. It is marvellous to see him treat his bruises in a matter-of-fact way and soothe away any aches and discomforts.

If children are old enough and are drawn to learning Reiki for themselves, they can enjoy the benefits for themselves. Some Reiki Masters occasionally offer classes for younger teenagers who prefer to be taught in a peer group. We taught such a group and look forward to receiving feedback from them in the future.

Children can be taught to meditate too. Starting with just five minutes a day, early in the morning, can bring many benefits. If the location has a tranquil atmosphere, the meditation can become a special time that can have a very calming effect and help the child to stay centred throughout the day. It might be the beginning of a lifelong habit and become a source of great peace for the child.

Babies and children very much enjoy receiving Reiki and it is useful for soothing the aches and pains that arise. Reiki also supports the healing in the case of serious illness as well as minor problems on a day-to-day basis. It is a very loving, nurturing way of caring for a baby and will intensify the relationship between the mother and the child. From soothing any colic that a baby might experience to reducing teething discomfort, Reiki can be helpful to ease pain and reduce inflammation. Treatment of babies and children generally does not take very long and a few moments can be enough. Absent healing can help an apprehensive child or soothe a crying baby in another room. As babies grow into children, Reiki is a wonderful way to nurture them.

## Reiki and Nightmares

Reiki can help ease many of childhood's difficult times especially in conjunction with visualization. One way of helping a child to regain confidence after experiencing a nightmare would be to comfort the child and when he or she is feeling safe and secure; place one hand on the child's forehead and another on the solar plexus area and allow the energy to flow. At the same time, it may be helpful to use the following visualization to help the child overcome the feelings of fear and helplessness that the nightmare has caused.

### Visualisation Following Nightmares
(Adapted from *Creative Vizualizations With Children* by Jennifer Day which is an excellent book for guiding children to creatively address the challenges that face them.

You are in a very safe place and there is love all around you. Very safe, peaceful and comforting. As you look around you in this very safe, peaceful place, you can see that monster (or whatever the child fears) and because you are in such a safe, peaceful place, you are in control of everything that happens here. As you look at the monster, you feel yourself becoming larger and larger and as you look at the monster, you can see that it is becoming smaller and smaller, until it is so small, it is small enough to play with. The monster is now so small, it is the size of a toy and you can play with it, roll it around or play a game with it. And if you want it to go away, you can throw it up in the air where it will travel far away to outer space and never return again.

## Reiki and Dreams

It is never advisable to interpret anyone else's dreams. However you can use Reiki to help yourself or someone else to understand their own dreams. We often have dreams which symbolize our current circumstances and understanding them can clarify our perspective. Often the elements in a dream can represent different aspects of ourselves. We have many facets to our complex personalities and, whilst resting or dreaming, our subconscious mind can re-enact a particular scenario that represents in symbol form, the situation that we find ourselves in.

To open the dream, there are three questions that you may ask yourself or another person to begin to gain some clarity as to its meaning.

- How did you feel in the dream? i.e. sad, happy, fearful, distressed, angry etc.
- How would you have liked the dream to end?
- Can you relate the dream to any particular situation in your everyday life?

Before giving yourself a Reiki treatment, you can set the intent that you will either experience that dream again or better still, that you will know by the end of the treatment or by the following day, what the dream may mean. It is surprising how many times the answer will come to you in this way.

## Reiki and Feng Shui

'There must be more to life than having everything.'

*Maurice Sendak*

The most common reaction to giving oneself a daily Reiki treatment at First Degree level is 'I can never find that sort of time' or 'I simply don't have a spare hour – or a spare five minutes'.

It is a sad fact of modern life that even with all kinds of appliances designed to save our time, we find we are even busier than ever. Our cupboards overflow with time-saving gadgets, we have devices to enable us to cook faster, wash and dry our clothes, clean our plates, reheat faster, boil faster, help us to lose weight faster, entertain us and we still haven't time to enjoy the sunset.

The truth is we have been so busy amassing all the things we believe we need in order to enjoy life more and to free up our time, that we haven't noticed that our lives are becoming more and more fragmented as we cram in, as much as we can, into each moment. It's no wonder that stress related disorders are becoming increasingly commonplace.

There are many excellent books written on the oriental art of Feng Shui. A vast subject best known for the art of furniture placement. Practitioners assess how to maximize the flow of energy through one's home through the design of the space and the arrangement of the contents.

Less known is space clearing, another aspect of Feng Shui. Sometimes it is possible, for a number of reasons, for energy to become stuck in a particular room or area and through various procedures it is a simple matter to clear it away.

Additionally Reiki Second Degree can be used effectively to energetically cleanse a room. The room actually feels better with technical disturbances being substantially reduced or even completely removed.

Reiki can often help us to dispose of our inner clutter by connecting us to our insight and inner wisdom. If however, we are always far too tired to bring changes into our lives, it will not always serve to assist us. If we can simplify our lives, we can relax more. It is up to us to dispose of our outer clutter so that we have the space for inner tranquillity.

In our homes, we often amass a far greater quantity of items than we are able to use. Our homes are full of clutter: out of date magazines, cassettes that are never listened to, unwanted gifts lurking at the back of cupboards as do kitchen gadgets, and old crockery, toys and games that no one will ever play with again and so on.

There are so many charities that will come and collect household paraphernalia and yet we often hang on to it all, in case we might need it in the future. If we were to clear it all out, recycle it and just keep what we are using right now, the home would be simpler to maintain.

A wise man once observed that if we were meant to be so frenetically busy all the time, we would have been called 'human doings'. By simplifying our lives in whatever ways we see fit, we can enjoy far more harmony and inner balance. For further information, read *Simplicity* by Elaine St James – if time permits.

## Food and Reiki

Cooked food can be enhanced by treating it with Reiki. Raw food is full of live enzymes and has an abundance of life force energy flowing through it. Cooked and pre-packaged meals low in life force can benefit greatly from the Reiki energy, as does microwaved food.

## Abundance and Prosperity Programming

Often it is our belief patterns that keep us from experiencing the abundance we desire. Money is simply another form of energy and in itself is neither positive nor negative. We can attract to ourselves whatever we require once we explore and breakthrough self-imposed barriers to abundance. Paula Horan has written an excellent book called *Abundance Through Reiki* which describes a self-help programme that explores belief patterns and promotes your own natural ability to experience creativity, freedom and abundance.

## Reiki to Increase Self-confidence

Whilst giving yourself a self-treatment, you can heal unwanted habits at the same time or simply boost your self esteem.

The following can be adapted for your personal use and recorded onto a cassette or you can ask someone to simply read it aloud to you during a Reiki treatment.

*Intent:* Set your intent for the Reiki energy to enhance your self confidence.

*Reiki Positions*

All the head positions, the heart, solar plexus, abdomen and pelvic areas.

> Find a comfortable position and begin to relax. Take a few deep breaths and feel yourself breathing in relaxation and breathing out tension. With every breath that you take in, feel yourself relax more and more. Imagine you are in a beautiful place in nature, a place where you feel calm and tranquil. Really feel yourself there. Take a look around you in your special place and notice the landscape. As you relax in your special place, feel all tension slipping away. Allow your body

to become more and more relaxed. As your body relaxes and all tension slips away, your mind begins to relax. As your mind begins to relax, you begin to feel more and more calm and every time you breathe in, allow yourself to become even more relaxed.

When you feel calm and relaxed, you feel more confident. More confident about yourself and more confident about what you are doing, more confident to be yourself and get the most out of life. Allow yourself to recall a time when you felt really confident. Perhaps it was when you were part of a winning team or when you received an award. Really feel this confidence. Enjoy this feeling of confidence. And you will find when this session is over, that you will take with you this peace, relaxation and confidence that you have now and it will stay with you and grow day by day. You will find you are more relaxed whatever you are doing and you'll be a more calm, more confident person. This will grow as each day goes by and you will find you are more free to be yourself and to enjoy life to the full.

## Weight Loss

*Intent:* Set your intent for the Reiki energy to assist you in losing weight.

### Reiki Positions

All the head positions, the heart, solar plexus, abdomen and pelvic areas concentrating especially on the throat position.

Find a comfortable position and begin to relax. Take a few deep breaths and see yourself breathing in a beautiful, healing coloured mist. As you breathe in this beautiful coloured mist, feel yourself relax completely and imagine that every time you breathe in this coloured mist, it is relaxing you more and more.

Imagine you are in a beautiful place in nature, a place where you feel calm safe and tranquil. Use all your senses to really feel yourself there. And every time you breathe in, allow yourself to become more and more relaxed.

As you relax in your special place, feel any tension slipping away. Allow your body to become even more relaxed. As your body relaxes and all tension slips away, your mind begins to relax. As your mind begins to relax, you begin to feel more calm and at ease.

And as you relax, you know you can achieve your goal. From now on you will find you will only desire healthy food, food which will help you to achieve your goal. When you are shopping, you will only notice fresh, healthy foods. Every healthy meal will take you closer to your goal and you won't be tempted to eat between meals. There will be times when you may be tempted to eat unhealthy food knowing that every time you refuse, you will be closer to your goal. This will make you very pleased and proud. Should there be any times when you are tempted to eat between meals, decide to drink a full glass of water. You will find this will fill you and you will feel satisfied.

As you feel relaxed and at ease, imagine yourself at your ideal weight. See yourself looking in the mirror at yourself, feeling pleased and proud that you have achieved your ideal weight. This will help to strengthen your resolve even more. After this session is over, you will find you take this resolve and confidence with you, and it will help you to achieve your goal.

## Becoming a Non-smoker

*Intent:* Set your intent for the Reiki energy to assist you to stop smoking.

*Reiki Positions*
All the head positions, the heart, solar plexus, abdomen, pelvic areas and shoulders.

Find a comfortable position and begin to relax. Take a few deep breaths and imagine a white shimmering star above your head. As you breathe in, imagine white light streaming out from this star filling your body with peace and relaxation. Every time that you breathe in, this white shimmering light fills you with relaxation.

Imagine you are in a beautiful place in nature, a place where you feel calm, safe and tranquil. Use all your senses to really feel yourself there. And every time you breathe in, allow yourself to become even more relaxed.

As you relax feel all tension slipping away. As your body relaxes and all tension slips away, your mind begins to relax. As your mind begins to relax, you begin to feel even more at ease and every time you breathe in, you feel more and more relaxed.

And as you feel relaxed, you know you can achieve the goal you have set yourself. You want to stop smoking and you can do it. From now on if you are offered a cigarette, say automatically 'No thank you, I am a non-smoker' and you will feel pleased and proud that you have refused because you will be breaking a habit that enslaves millions.

There will be times when you may be tempted to smoke and at these times all you need to do is to take a deep and comfortable breath of fresh air. Even now, as you think these words, you can breathe in . . . hold your breath for a few seconds . . . and as you exhale . . . you let go of tension, let go of cravings and relax. Each time this happens you will feel very pleased and proud because you are achieving your goal. Whenever you finish a meal, you know you can remind yourself of your decision to be a non-smoker. Every time you wash your hands you know you are washing away an old habit, washing away unhealthiness and you congratulate yourself on your continuing decision to remain a non smoker.

You may wish to include a substitute food or drink to assist you such as eating an apple or drinking water and this could be incorporated into the visualization by suggesting to yourself that you will enjoy choosing to eat/drink (*insert your substitute*) at (*insert all the particular times or occasions you normally smoke*) which will be enjoyable and satisfying.

The above can be adapted infinitely to suit different situations and you can choose different imagery and choose different backgrounds too, such as beautiful lakes, beaches, meadows, woodlands, gardens or wherever you prefer. You can change the wording to deal with stress, fear or anything else you prefer. If you have two cassette players you can play Reiki music as well so that you have a tranquil background. The possibilities are endless.

## Reiki and Rejuvenation

Whilst Reiki cannot perform instant miracles of rejuvenation, regular treatment ensures efficient toxic elimination, improves circulation and combined with nutrition that energizes rather than depletes the system, serves to keep the skin radiant and healthy. Treating yourself with Reiki is also more effective and less expensive than many of the creams, potions and miracle drugs that are available. Keeping healthy requires taking on a considerable amount of personal responsibility for oneself.

# CHAPTER EIGHT
# REIKI WITH CHRONIC ILLNESS

Reiki can be extremely helpful when treating the very ill, the infirm and the terminally ill as well as benefiting their families and those taking care of them. The carers can always use Reiki to replenish their own energy levels so that they are more able to provide the support and healing for others. Reiki can be used for pain relief and to provide a nurturing, reassuring connection between the person and those in a caring capacity.

Dr Elisabeth Kubler-Ross pioneered remarkable research with terminally ill patients ultimately changing forever our perceptions on this aspect of human experience.

Whilst nearly all religions and sages from many cultures have talked of the immortality of the human soul, the subject of death is not something our civilization is able to talk about easily. Dr Kubler-Ross encouraged patients to talk about their feelings and discovered that they all shared a tremendous feeling of isolation as well as fear and often anger too. With her compassion and warm understanding, Dr Kubler Ross inspired countless medical staff, care workers and families of terminally ill patients to provide sensitive, responsive care so that it was possible for each person to die in dignity surrounded by love.

Princess Diana touched the hearts of millions with her compassion for those who were suffering. Her hospital visits changed the lives of those she visited forever. She had a rare gift of being able to communicate her empathy with people regardless of their illness or their circumstances. She always physically touched those she visited, even if they suffered from a disease that was considered contagious or dangerous in some way. Whether Princess Diana had ever taken Reiki training is not known, but her instinctive ability to touch and bring comfort to others in pain demonstrates the important element of human touch as used in Reiki.

Many people who have had 'near death experiences' have described remarkably similar journeys towards a bright light.

They have nearly all met people whom they either once knew or who were specifically there to accompany them. Yet despite copious amounts of data recording such encounters, many people die alone in great fear.

Experience with our own parents as described in the preface of this book taught us much about the nature of caring for terminally ill people. Since discovering Reiki, we have learned there is a great difference between healing and curing. Sometimes, there simply isn't a cure. Healing can be used and that person may pass away truly at peace with themselves and others, surrounded by their loved ones.

Dr Kubler-Ross defined five stages between the initial reaction of an individual to a diagnosis and the final acceptance of the inevitable. When assisted compassionately throughout, the process becomes considerably easier and could result in that person finding a tremendous amount of peace and harmony that could assist them and all those connected with them to find strength and clarity during a difficult time.

She has written several books on this subject. The following stages are taken from her book *Death and Dying.*

### 1. *Denial and isolation*
Denial is very often the initial reaction of those who are informed as to the terminal nature of their illness. Patients become convinced 'there must have been a mistake – the X-rays must be mixed up'. Dr Kubler-Ross believes that this reaction is one of shock that allows the person time to come to terms with the unexpectedly frightening news and suggests it is helpful if the support given during this period allows the individual time to adjust to the diagnosis. Reiki can be very helpful to treat the shock as well as any symptoms. As mentioned earlier in the book, there are times when Reiki is not appropriate (see Chapter 5).

### 2. *Anger*
The second reaction, after the diagnosis has been accepted, is one of anger and resentment. 'Why me?' 'Why at this time?'. This stage is usually much more difficult to deal with from the family's viewpoint. Dr Kubler-Ross believes it is important to empathize with the person at this time and be understanding about their predicament. Reiki can be helpful

to alleviate any discomfort and reduce the side effects of any treatment that is prescribed.

3. *Bargaining*

Following the stage of anger, Dr Kubler-Ross observed that often people will subsequently react by bargaining for more time such as saying 'If I can just be around for my son's wedding' or 'if only I could be here for the birth of my first grandchild'. Sometimes patients promise if they can have longer they will dedicate their lives to God.

Dr Kubler-Ross suggests it would be helpful if these remarks were not just brushed aside by staff, but taken as the beginning of a discussion about any guilt or regret the person may be experiencing at this time in their life.

4. *Depression*

Depression is often the next stage when their situation becomes more difficult and they must endure more surgery or more discomfort. There may also be financial burdens that must be faced.

An understanding person will have no difficulty in establishing the cause of the depression. Reiki may help to deal with the grief that the person is experiencing in order to prepare themselves for the next stage; that of separation from their loved ones.

It is helpful for the person to be assisted in concluding any unfinished business and resolving any conflicts that remain between themselves and their families or other persons close to them.

Reiki can often help with any pain relief or to speed up the healing process after surgery has taken place. Additionally Reiki can effectively increase clarity so that the person can become aware of what needs to be done and is able to resolve any remaining difficulties.

5. *Acceptance*

If a person has been given enough time and some help in working through the other stages, he or she will become neither angry nor depressed and will reach a stage of acceptance of the inevitable.

This is not necessarily a happier stage. It is a time when the patient will have found some peace and acceptance and could also be a time when the rest of the family may themselves be in more need of help and assistance.

Often the patient wishes to be left alone at this stage and not be bothered by the outside world. It may be helpful to visit in silence and show that the person is not alone and is really cared about and supported. Reiki may or may not be refused and the patient could benefit from distant healing at this time. Throughout all these stages hope persists. Even the most accepting patient hopes that a last-minute cure may avail itself.

When finally there is a time in the patient's life when the pain ceases and the mind drifts off into a dreamless state, it becomes more difficult for the next of kin to know whether to care for the dying or to attend the needs of the living. Dr Kubler-Ross suggests that the carer could be of great help at this time by selecting the person who feels most comfortable to stay with the dying person. This allows the others to return home without feeling they are abandoning the patient to die alone.

If the person is unconscious, they may still be able to benefit from the Reiki energy and if they are close to death, they may find they can use the energy to assist them in their transition.

In conclusion, Reiki can provide a gentle and effective means of supporting and helping our loved ones who are very unwell or terminally ill. Reiki also allows one to experience a sense of union with the dying person and assists them to come to terms with their situation.

> For what is it to die but to stand naked in the wind and to melt into the sun?
> And what is it to cease breathing but to free the breath from its restless tides, that it may rise and expand and seek God unencumbered?
>
> Only when you drink from the river of silence shall you indeed sing.
> And when you have reached the mountain top, then you shall begin to climb.
> And when the earth shall claim your limbs, then shall you truly dance.

Extract from *Death* by Khalil Gibran

## When Reiki Doesn't Seem to Work

One of the things that Reiki does teach you is tremendous detachment. You become a channel for the energy, allowing the energy to flow through you as you make it available for other people. It is appropriate that you allow the other person to do with that energy whatever they choose, without being attached to the outcome. That is why it is important to allow someone else to ask you for a Reiki treatment.

Persons who come for a treatment because they have been persuaded to, or who may have simply come along to prove that something like Reiki couldn't possibly work at all, will to some extent block the effectiveness of the Reiki energy because of their own resistance.

The results of Reiki treatments are unpredictable and expectations may not be promptly fulfilled. As Reiki channels, we are merely observers and can never permit ourselves to become judgmental should the desired outcome not be achieved.

Sometimes the person may lose too many secondary benefits if his or her symptoms are removed. However much the individual may assure you they wish to get well, they may be receiving an exceptional amount of attention from their families whilst unwell, which they might be unwilling to give up should their symptoms be removed. At an unconscious level, they may be resisting healing.

One such person who came for healing had forged a marvellous relationship with his previously distant father whilst confined to a wheelchair with post viral fatigue syndrome. It was clear he was unwilling to risk losing this warm relationship by being able to regain the use of his legs and he soon stopped treatment.

Another lady during an illness was able to adopt a strong role within the hierarchy of her family that she was reluctant to relinquish. No method of healing would have succeeded during this time. At an unconscious level, she was choosing illness rather than health.

Some individuals have strong opinions which would prevent them benefiting from a remedy which falls outside their accepted belief system. It is important they are able to freely choose their own method of healing. Reiki simply may not be right for them and they may not believe that such a spiritual form of treatment could remove their symptoms. That is their right and Reiki is simply not a suitable form of treatment for some people.

These examples are unusual. It is however helpful to be aware of the possibility of such situations occurring. The majority of situations provide marvellous and often unexpected opportunities for growth and fulfilment for both the person being treated and the healer.

# CHAPTER NINE
# REIKI FOR SELF-DEVELOPMENT AND SPIRITUAL GROWTH

'We are not human beings having a spiritual experience.
We are spiritual beings having a human experience.'

*Teilhard de Chardin*

Reiki enhances our inner spiritual connection. We begin to respond differently, simply becoming more open and loving. Additionally intuition develops and we are able to tap into inner wisdom and guidance. Personal and spiritual growth is heightened and a multitude of possibilities for accelerating personal growth begin to emerge. It is possible to learn to sense subtle energies and develop awareness beyond our five senses and potentially enter expanded states of consciousness where we can discover inner joy, peace and vitality.

Meditation is probably the simplest way to expand consciousness and tune in to your inner guidance. It is highly likely that giving or receiving Reiki enables you to enter a meditative state without realizing it. Those who already meditate find their meditations deepen following Reiki attunements. Reiki and meditation complement each other.

Meditating for just 20 minutes a day can be an invaluable way of discovering inner peace and accessing your internal source of inspiration.

*Meditation Exercise*
Sit comfortably upright on a chair, close your eyes and allow yourself to take several slow deep breaths. Begin to focus all your attention on your breathing, becoming aware of the rhythms of your breath as you breathe in and out. Keep your awareness on your breathing without thinking too much about it, observing the flow of your breathing. Allow passing thoughts

to drift by without involving you too much. If your mind should wander, just gently bring your attention back to your breathing. After about 20 minutes you may find that your mind becomes very still and you are able to access a very calm state of being. This may take some practise and you may find you wish to focus your attention on a single word, sound or mantra instead of breathing. Sometimes, it is necessary to experiment to find what works for you. There is no right or wrong way to meditate. Try and find the method that suits you.

Meditating for about 20 minutes, twice a day, is ideal if you can find the time. If you are an early riser, sunrise is a good time to meditate, especially if busy family life prevents you doing so around breakfast time. Similarly, close to sunset is another time that works well. Both these times herald the change between day and night, which is a special time providing an invaluable space before the day unfolds or the night arrives. When you have meditated for some time, you can find that you slip into a wonderful space where the mind becomes as still as a forest pool. The nature of reality and ultimate truth begin to unfold and it is possible to find great peace and inner strength.

Visualization can be helpful as well. Various forms of visualization are often used on personal development courses and can be used during Reiki training. During Reiki attunements, participants often experience overwhelming feelings of love and a sense of being connected to all living things. The feeling of love is not of an interpersonal nature, it is more in the realm of universal love.

Whilst Reiki is a route by which to enter expanded states of awareness, visualization can pave the way to higher levels of mind. Through visualization, we are able to access that wiser all-knowing part of ourselves, that is often called the Higher Self. Whilst we often struggle with a particular issue, our Higher Self has a perception of the whole picture and can sense the outcome of a situation. By integrating this expansive aspect of ourselves, we can often access this knowledge and draw inspiration and clarity from a greater perspective.

The following visualization is a journey to connect with the Higher Self, in order to experience a higher state of mind. Guided imagery is much more effective if you are in a relaxed state of mind. Be open to whatever might happen during this inner journey and trust that whatever happens is right for you.

You may choose to have someone read this to you as you relax, or record it onto a tape player.

*Journey to the Higher Self*
Imagine you are on a special journey to find your Higher Self. You are feeling very relaxed as you float gently on in darkness travelling deeper and deeper into space. As you continue to move deeper into the darkness of inner space, you become aware of a flow of warmth that is drawn towards you and as this flow of healing warmth travels closer to you, it is as if you being gently enveloped in a gossamer wave of pure love.

It is your Higher Self, that part from which you were created, the wiser all-knowing centre of your essence, which gently cocoons you in a flow of healing energy, giving you strength and unity, wholeness and harmony. Feel this flow of warmth as it releases all your stresses and strains, allowing energy to flow freely through your system. Allow this energy to flow through every part of you, at every level. Feel the warmth of the love, as you feel the power of the healing energy flowing through to you from your Higher Self. Know too, that the wisdom of the Higher Self is also flowing through to you too, filling every part of you at every level.

As the healing energy flows into your being, allow yourself to relax completely and totally, letting your Higher Self replenish your system with whatever you need. Feel the wholeness and harmony fill you with peace and tranquillity. When you are ready slowly and gently return to the room.

## Using Reiki to Solve Problems and Achieve Goals

An interesting technique for problem solving is to use internal advisors or inner guides created by using the power of our imagination. Such helpers can range from Reiki guides, wise sages, figures from history, present day experts in a particular field or any characters at all, real or imaginary. After a little practise, imaginary conversations can be held and it is possible to receive assistance which can be very helpful. Books and workshops describing the Silva Mind Control method have included such methods.

Through visualization, we can establish a connection to such inner counsellors. Surprisingly, the characters do become increasingly real as time goes by, and can be a marvellous resource for resolving issues. Of course it is possible to access our inner advisors in any setting at all, and the following meditation is just an example to start the process.

### Meeting Your Advisors

Relax deeply and imagine yourself in a beautiful place in nature. Use all your senses to imagine yourself there. Visualize yourself raising your cupped hands in front of you, and sending energy streaming out from your hands. From this energy, see a stream of light form a bridge of white light in front of you. Begin walking over the bridge and as you walk across, allow all tension to disappear and feel yourself filled with relaxation and tranquillity. At the other side of the bridge are some steps leading up a gently sloping hillside. Take the steps to the top where you will come to a beautiful, shimmering temple surrounded by fragrant, colourful gardens. Standing in the gardens are your advisors, waiting to welcome you. Greet them and spend the next few moments asking for their guidance on any subject at all. You may wish to ask for insight on a particular problem or advice as to the next step in your life's journey or perhaps about skills and qualities you wish to develop. Listen carefully for the answers. Spend as much time as you wish with your guides, and know that you can return here whenever you wish. When you have finished, gently return down the steps, across the bridge of light and bring yourself back to the room.

### Obtaining Answers to Questions

This is another useful technique for receiving answers to questions from your inner guidance resource, if you possess an alarm clock with a 'sleep' button you can press when initially awoken, that allows you to sleep for another ten minutes or so before ringing again. When the alarm first rings, pose the question you have in mind to a Reiki guide or another internal advisor, press the sleep button and let yourself fall asleep again. By the time the alarm rings again, you should have your answer. The early hours are an excellent time to access inner clarification, which is why meditating at or after sunrise is so appropriate. The mind has usually had time to clear out all the less meaningful thoughts relating to the daily humdrum of our lives, resulting in more significant images and ideas being allowed to surface in the early hours.

# PART THREE
# REIKI TRAINING

# CHAPTER TEN
# THE FIRST DEGREE CLASS

There are three levels of energy in the Usui System of Reiki. The first being the introductory level or Reiki First Degree as it is generally known. The next level of Reiki is known as Reiki Second Degree and the final level of energy is the Master level of Reiki energy.

First Degree Reiki training is made up of four sessions usually with one attunement per session. These sessions often take place over a two day period, and can be over a weekend, or alternatively can be held over four evenings. Each Reiki Master will bring his or her own variations to this basic structure. Mrs Takata, the lady responsible for bringing the Usui System of Reiki to the West, taught the four sessions over four consecutive days or evenings and whilst the time scales may vary today, the format of the training remains virtually the same as it was, when she taught Reiki.

Certain other aspects of the training also remain the same and follow a specific form such as the four attunements, the telling of the Reiki story, the five ethical principles, the hand positions, instructions for self-treatment, the treatment of others and the treatment of injury.

The remaining components of the workshop rely very much on the personality, ability and interests of the particular Reiki Master. There may even be variations between the classes any one Reiki Master holds, depending on the particular group energy of the participants.

At each First Degree class, there should be four attunements or initiations for each participant, usually two per day in the case of a weekend class, for example. The training should never be held on one day only as time is needed to integrate the experience. Nor is it appropriate for Second Degree training to directly follow the First Degree class as a great period of growth is triggered following the attunements at First Degree level. It is very important that time is available to allow each person to assimilate both the new level of awareness that emerges, and the increased energy.

Some Reiki Masters recommend participants have no heavy meals, drugs or alcoholic drinks over the three-day period prior to and following training (with the exception of prescribed medication). Smaller classes are preferable with approximately 12 to 15 participants per class (although larger classes are acceptable if there is more than one Reiki Master present). It is important that each participant is able to receive personal attention from a Reiki Master.

A typical format for the first day may include two of the four attunements. Additionally, the history of Reiki including the five ethical principles are covered and full details of how to give yourself a self-treatment with instructions for the 21 or even 30 day cleansing period. We usually recommend a 30-day self-treatment period. We often advise participants to start keeping a journal to observe the changes that occur over this period and subsequently. As well as connecting to the energy on the first day, students may also become acquainted with the universal principles of energy flow so that they are able to direct the energy to where it is required in their lives.

On the second day, the third and fourth attunement takes place. There may also be tools and techniques for using Reiki not only for healing but also as a path for personal and spiritual growth. Participants are usually taught how to give a Reiki treatment to others (see Chapter 5). Details of how to develop intuitive and kinaesthetic sensitivity as well as practical knowledge for setting up a treatment room may be given. In addition, other information such as using Reiki to help people through a difficult period in their lives, as well as being able to recognize and support them through a healing crisis may be included. This is usually followed by a practical one-to-one session when all participants give and receive a full Reiki treatment. There should be plenty of time for questions and answers throughout the training and ample opportunity for sharing any experiences that may have occurred.

Reiki is an oral tradition and there is usually no need to take notes at any point. There is normally a considerable difference in the students from when they arrive to when they depart. They are usually initially quiet, reserved and sometimes tense. The

First Degree initiations are said to open the heart, hand and the crown chakras and the energies that flow through their systems invariably have a transformational effect. Everyone leaves feeling light hearted, relaxed and loving.

Some people have deeply moving spiritual experiences during the attunements and others feel deeply relaxed though not aware of any significant occurrence.

We are often asked why Reiki training is divided into three stages. This is because in Dr Usui's day, students would travel with him, learning and practising Reiki until eventually they too were ready to teach. This is not a practical option today and in modern times, it is simply easier to divide the attunements into degrees to allow the necessary time to assimilate the various levels of energy amplification.

The attunement is a very special time and experience in which the student may become conscious of an inner world unfolding. We advise each person to close their eyes, as all that is happening is usually seen from within. As in meditation, it is best not to be distracted by the external physical world. It is a time in which to enjoy the energy from an inner perspective.

## Bringing Change Into Your Life

Following the attunements, a number of changes may occur as a result of the increased flow of life force energy. The vibratory rate of each individual is raised and although changes are subtle, the overall difference may bring considerable change into the lives of participants. Some changes may include:

- Becoming more intuitively aware and generally more sensitive to energies. This continues to develop especially when the energy is being channelled either during a self-treatment or when treating others.

- Becoming more responsive and loving as the heart chakra opens. The energy allows you to become more aware of your feelings and emotions. Subsequently you become more sensitive to your own needs, as well as to the needs of others.

- Increased awareness and clarity leading to a shift in perception. The mind becomes clearer and often our decision-making process is altered allowing more solutions to surface and more flexibility in resolving issues.

Other changes may be noticed such as:

- Changes in diet often showing a preference for food that carries a finer, lighter vibration. Often people decide to reduce the amount of red meat eaten or to increase the amount of vegetarian or even raw food in the diet. Heavier cooked food may lose some of its appeal.

- Overcoming eating or other habit disorders. Many people have simply stopped smoking after taking Reiki training. Sometimes they have said they no longer need a 'smoke screen' between themselves and the world. Similarly, those suffering from eating disorders have found themselves feeling more balanced and centred.

- Improved focus, memory and concentration. Many students have reported improvement to their concentration span. Even their meditations have deepened since the Reiki attunements.

- A different response from family members, friends, colleagues, pets etc., may be observed. After taking First Degree, many people have noticed that stray pets come up to them in the park and strangers in the supermarket start engaging them in conversation.

- New interests emerge. Many people decide to take up new interests, discover talents they were unaware of, or unexpectedly change their jobs, or even their professions.

## The Five Ethical Principles

Dr Usui developed the five ethical principles (see Chapter 2) as he realized the importance of a person's participation in his or her own healing process. A person needed to ask for help and be active in bringing change into his or her life. He appreciated that healing the spirit was paramount and this required commitment and a degree of personal responsibility to be effective. These guidelines were developed to help people to grow and change and are as relevant today as when they were developed. These principles may vary slightly according to each Reiki Master.

### Just for Today, Do Not Worry

This is to remind people that there is a divine purpose to everything and without awareness of this, further limitations may be created. Taoist sages declare that 'any event in itself is neither good nor bad, it simply is'. Energy used for worrying is in essence wasted, as it brings no change to a situation. Dr Usui in this principle was reminding people of the importance of trust. We live in a responsive universe and as long as we are clear as to what we want, our needs will be met. It is important to simply trust that things will work out for the best in the end. What is beyond our control cannot be changed and squandering copious amount of our energy on worrying, may only serve to diminish our vitality and cloud our perception.

## Just for Today, Do Not Anger

When a situation does not live up to our expectations, we become angry. Anger is a destructive emotion when expressed inappropriately. Anger can also be a powerful motivator for change, provided it is possible to become consciously aware of your reactions and take charge of your emotions. It would be inappropriate to feel guilt if anger arises as it is a natural reaction to have, as long as it does not lead us into becoming judgmental which is not helpful to anyone. Anger creates disharmony within the body. Dr Usui was not asking people to deny their feelings. Instead he was asking them to respond with love.

## Earn Your Living Honestly

A sage was once asked to explain how it was possible to gauge how prosperous a person was. He thought for a moment and replied that the measure of how prosperous a person was, depended upon the amount of peace they could carry in their heart. When a person earned their living honestly, they are not only being honest with others, they are being honest with themselves. They trust in their own abilities to create the abundance they need, to provide for themselves and their families. Such persons would indeed carry more peace in their hearts and would be immeasurably well-off. Dr Usui, in creating this principle was aware that dishonesty was a heavy burden to carry and that individuals could align themselves more fully with their life's purpose and their creativity, if they were to earn their living honestly.

## Show Gratitude to Every Living Thing

Gratitude allows us to open to the fruits of the universe and create a conscious awareness that magnetically attracts abundance and repels lack. There is a well-known universal principle that 'like attracts like'. Dr Usui knew that feeling and showing gratitude could enable people to bring success, prosperity and happiness into their lives.

*Honour Your Parents, Teachers and Elders*

This principle of showing love and respect for our parents, teachers and elders may well be extended to every living thing. All living things are interdependent. Man's inhumanities to his fellow man and to the environment have caused many humanitarian and ecological problems. In order for the planet as a whole to survive, it has become apparent that we must change. Dr Usui appreciated that our growth and indeed our survival depended on loving actions, respect for one another and all living things. The first place to start is with our loved ones and those close to us. Taking positive action and responding sensitively with warmth and compassion towards parents, teachers, elders and subsequently everyone you encounter from now on, will go some way towards reducing the suffering in the world around us.

## The Importance of an Energy Exchange

Dr Usui's experience in the beggars' quarters in Kyoto taught him the importance of an exchange of energy for the healer's time (see Chapter 2). His initial intention was to give away healing to those in need so that they could eventually support themselves and become responsible citizens. He discovered that many of the beggars he had helped returned after some time to the beggars' quarters, having rejected the jobs he had helped them to find, and the life in the city, because they didn't want the responsibility of caring for themselves.

He came to understand the importance of allowing a person to ask for healing. He also appreciated that it wasn't right to keep someone feeling indebted. People needed to give back what they had been given or life would be valueless. It was at that time he came to understand that the purpose of the symbols in his vision was to attune others, so that they could take responsibility for their own healing.

The exchange of energy does not always have to be in the form of money, it can be any form of exchange that is acceptable. Amongst close family members and friends, exchanges of energy are frequent anyway and specific requests are usually unnecessary.

To reduce the burden of obligation, an exchange of energy is an important part of the healing process. It is far better to treat people who are keen and willing to transform themselves than those not interested or prepared to receive.

For Reiki treatments, it is usually recommended that the charge is comparable to the cost of a body massage in your area. Most practitioners offer concessions to those unable to afford a treatment. Similarly, Reiki Masters usually offer reduced fees to students who wish to learn and are unable to afford all the tuition cost.

To live in balance and harmony, it is helpful to feel comfortable with the concept of giving and receiving, which is the essence of an exchange of energy.

## Giving a Reiki Treatment

Each of the hand positions has a specific significance and can provoke different reactions from both the healer and the person being treated. The person giving the treatment receives the energy running through their system and usually benefits from the treatment too. The energy heightens perception and sensitivities and is usually a very special time for both healer and recipient. There are many more hand positions and guidelines than the basic ones described here which are often taught at First Degree level. When giving first aid, it is usual to place hands directly onto the area that needs treating. Books have been written on specific hand positions for specific illnesses. Other positions may be discovered intuitively whilst giving a Reiki treatment. Flexibility is important overall and it is well to remember that Mrs Takata taught Reiki as an intuitive art not as a rigid system.

## How to Determine the Most Appropriate Hand Positions

Except for shock or accident, give Reiki to the entire body whenever possible, as the body is a complete unit and should be treated as a whole. If you only have a short space of time for treatment and can only do a limited number of hand positions, it is possible to determine where the best optimum positions are by:

- Directly treating the area of discomfort.
- Use intuitive abilities and trust that you will be able to discern where the energy is most needed.
- If you are familiar with acupuncture meridian points, give Reiki over the area that corresponds to the symptom.
- If you are familiar with reflexology points in hands and feet, give Reiki to the corresponding area.
- Observe where the other person receiving the treatment places their hands instinctively, this is often where it is most needed.

## Hand Positions for a Full Treatment

*First Position*

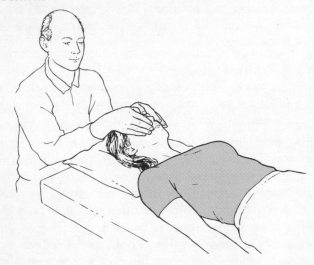

This first position is over the eyes, forehead and cheeks. This position affects the pituitary and pineal glands as well as the eyes, sinuses, nose, teeth and jaws. It also helps to reduce stress and help the processes of thought and concentration. This is also the natural position used to treat a headache and for colds of the nasal and frontal sinuses. It also assists in awakening the third eye.

*Second Position*

The second position with the palms of the hands over the temples, thumbs over the third eye, affects the brain and the eye

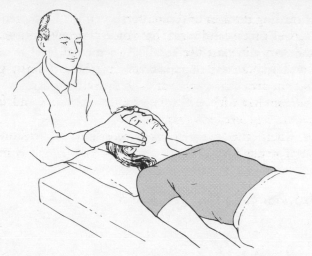

muscles. It is also good for colds as well as for headaches, seizures as well as the pituitary and pineal glands. It assists with shock and motion sickness as well as helping relieve worry, hysteria, stress and depression. This position helps to enhance dream and past life recall. It assists in creating calmness, helping to improve memory retention, productivity and creativity.

*Third Position*

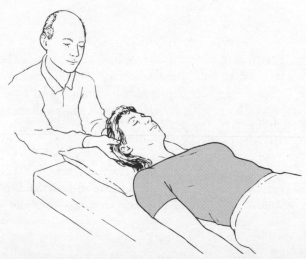

The third position with your hands at the back of the head and base of the skull, affects weight and vision. It assists with speech

113

and controls the nervous system for the entire body, relieves stress and enhances relaxation. It relieves pain, nausea and enhances dream and past life recall. At a mental level it calms thoughts and helps relieve depression.

*Fourth Position*

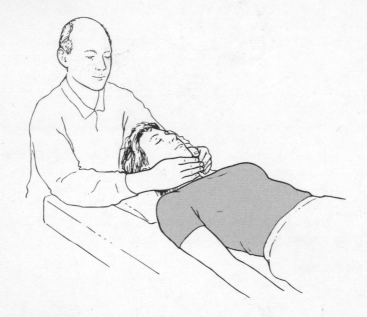

The fourth position is over the throat and along the jawline. It assists with strokes, tonsils, throat, larynx, thyroid, parathyroid and helps in balancing blood pressure both high and low. This position improves lymphatic drainage and brings calmness and clarity of thought. It helps the vocal cords, anorexia, metabolic diseases and weight problems. It also helps to bring confidence and joy as well as relieving anger, hostility and resentment. It is important not to touch the neck when treating.

*Fifth Position*

The fifth position over the heart, treats the heart, lungs and thymus which affect the immune system and circulation. At an emotional level this facilitates the release of stress and assists in enhancing the capacity to love and be loved. At a mental

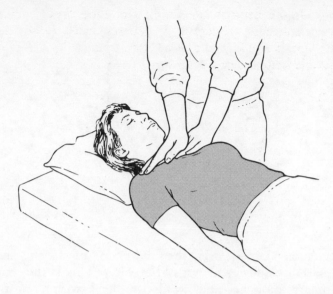

level, this relieves depression and helps to restore balance and harmony.

*Sixth Position*

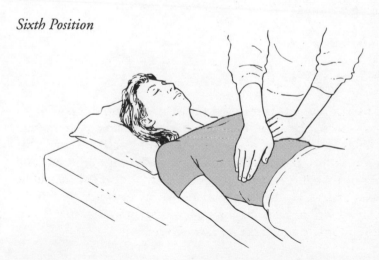

The sixth position just below the chest, still on the rib cage, is over the solar plexus area. This affects the liver, stomach, spleen, gall bladder and digestion. It also helps to bring relaxation and helps to release fears and stress. At a mental level, it helps bring about inner balance.

*Seventh Position*

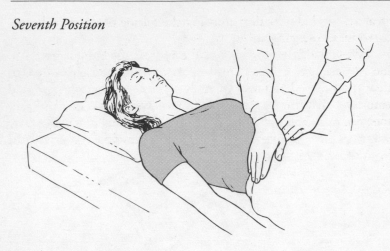

The seventh position over the abdomen affects the liver, pancreas, gall bladder and transverse colon. This is the centre where angry thoughts and words are held within creating feelings of bitterness, blame and frustration. Bringing energy to this area assists in releasing negative thoughts. This is a very calming position.

*Eighth Position*

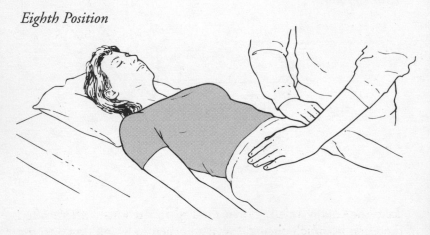

The eighth position is over the pelvic area. This affects lymphatic drainage and the release of toxins. Additionally it brings energy to the large and small intestines, the bladder, issues of constipation and diarrhoea, the ovaries, uterus and prostate. This centre relates to feelings of security and pleasure. It is also the area of creativity and elimination allowing the release of unneeded, out-dated ideas and substances.

Although this is not part of the basic Usui System guide to the 12 positions, at this point we usually take the hands down to treat the knees. The knees often store much anger and repressed emotions. Treating the knees for a moment or two is often very soothing and the hands may feel as if they really want to stay longer, which is a sign that this area is deriving much benefit from the energy.

*Knees and Feet Position*

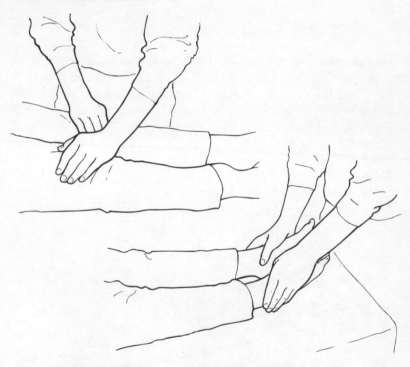

Take the energy briefly down the legs to the knees where often there can be much energy drawn and then move on down to the feet and place the hands over the ankles for a moment or two, working towards the toes. After this point, the person is asked to turn over. Even if they have been deeply asleep, it is amazing how they will wake up briefly to turn over and then drift straight back to sleep.

117

*Ninth Position*

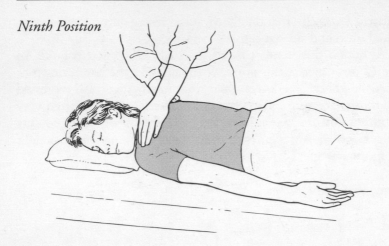

This position is at the top of the shoulders and affects the heart as well as the shoulders and the neck. It facilitates the release of stress and burdens and brings peace and harmony. This is the area where most tension is experienced, in and about the shoulder area, and gives rise to the feeling of 'carrying the weight of the world on the shoulders'.

*Tenth Position*

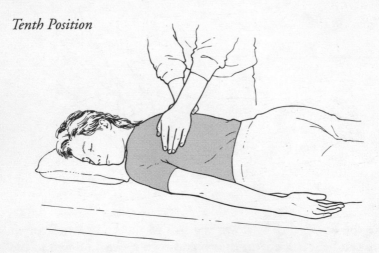

The tenth position is over the shoulder blades. This position affects the heart and the lungs at a physical level. At an emotional level it enhances the ability to love and be loved as well as facilitating the release of stress. At a mental level this position brings peace and harmony.

*Eleventh Position*

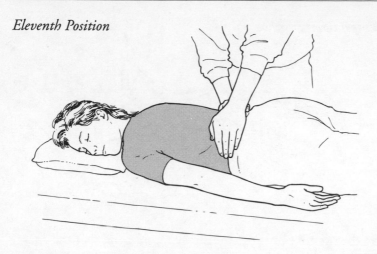

The eleventh position is over the lower back. This affects the gall bladder, pancreas, transverse colon as well as the adrenal glands, the kidneys and the lower back. It assists in releasing self-criticism, anxiety and negativity. It allows feelings of harmony and joy to surface.

*Twelfth Position*

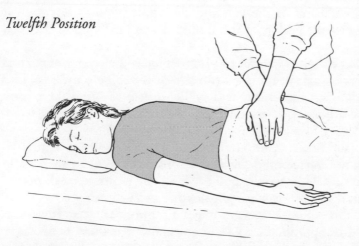

This position is over the tail bone and affects the large and small intestines, bladder, uterus, ovaries, prostate and coccyx. This is also the centre of creativity and releasing. Releasing old thoughts and feelings makes room for new innovative, creative expressions to emerge.

*Soles of the Feet Position*

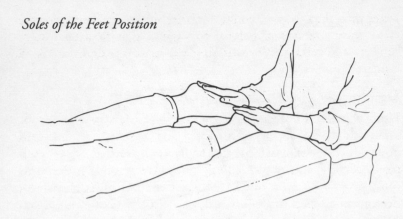

After the twelfth position, we usually recommend that the energy is taken very briefly down to treat the soles of the feet, benefiting the reflex zones. As many people will be driving after the session or certainly will need to be alert, it is helpful to briefly take the energy back up to the head. Place the hands in line at the base of the spine, one in front of the other with a gap of one hand's width in between. After a moment, move the hands up placing the lower hand in the gap and the upper hand in line with it higher up the back near the shoulders and finally up to the head itself.

After this, it is helpful to briefly smooth the energy out across the back with sweeping motions from the spine outwards. This is a different movement and will also help to bring the person round a little and remind them the treatment is coming to an end.

Finally, 'sweep the aura' free of any accumulated debris by using gentle sweeping movements from the head to the toes in the auric field above the body. We usually recommend disposing of this debris by visualizing it floating away.

At this point, the person may be coming round a little and it would be appropriate to let them know that there is no hurry and that you are leaving them for a brief moment to give them a moment or two to surface. This would be a good time to wash your hands and bring back a glass of water for both yourself and your client.

Allow a few moments for receiving response from the person being treated. It is best to advise them to drink much more water than they usually would, to assist any toxic release. For the same reason, it is also helpful to suggest that they take more showers and refrain from drinking alcohol over the next 24–48 hours.

## Developing Kinaesthetic Sensitivity

Using the hands to scan the body in order to receive impressions as to where the energy is most needed, can be a simple and powerful tool for assessing the energetic requirements of each person. The perception of energy can be very subtle initially for most people. As each one of us is different there is no way of determining when this will develop. It usually takes time, much practise and focus to develop this awareness, though it can be surprizing how quickly this ability grows.

### Sensing Energy

To sense energy, rub the hands briskly together and hold them about eighteen inches apart. Now bring the hands together very slowly noticing when there is slight resistance. This very subtle, intangible resistance is the energy. Keep trying until you can get a sense of it.

When you are giving Reiki treatments, your hands become your inner eyes and become trained to perceive the areas that need attention.

When you are comfortable with the above exercise and have a sense of what energy feels like, use the hands to scan the body to pick up any impressions you may receive. You might want to practise on family and friends initially prior to clients.

To scan the body, rub the hands briskly together and hold them over the person's head in the auric field over the body. Move them up higher and then lower to try to get an impression of where the energy field extends to. In a healthy person this should be well above the body. Then having ascertained the extent of the energy field, move the hands slowly across the auric field from the person's head to their feet. Notice any differences in heat, coolness, variations in the depth of the energetic field and any other impression that you are able to sense. This takes some practise. Don't worry if it doesn't happen immediately.

It is helpful to scan each person before their treatment to assess which areas need to be concentrated upon. It is important to scan once and once only, as it can be disconcerting to the person lying on the treatment table to have you go up and down their body repeatedly. It may well alarm them.

Provided the person knows generally what happens during treatment, it is not even vitally important to explain that you are scanning their body and hoping to receive impressions. It could be of concern to someone that you are spending much time over their heart for example, which might give them the idea that they are about to experience a heart attack. If you appear to be holding back on any impressions received, it may be feared that you are concealing vital information.

Having completed the body scan, go on to treat the body. Bear in mind any areas you feel are particularly important to concentrate on. Notice any particular sensations in the area that the person has requested you spend time on.

## Guide to the Meaning of Impressions Received

It would not be possible to definitively identify what personal impressions received during a body scan or treatment may mean. To assist in the development of such sensitivity, we have compiled a list of what such impressions, in our opinion, could mean.

### Visual Impressions

Sometimes visual impressions are received and these are usually the easiest to interpret. It may be appropriate to discuss them with the person, if you know them well, and feel they might be receptive. Otherwise, it may not be appropriate, helpful or in the person's best interest to mention images that could cause them to feel fearful or uneasy.

### Heat

This indicates that the energy is needed in this area and is being drawn. Sometimes the heat can be intense and it may even be necessary to break contact for a moment. This is unusual. One person was receiving Reiki for a headache. The practitioner's hands were placed on both sides of this person's head. He experienced warmth on the right hand side of his head only and was curious to know why this should be. When asked where his

122

headache was, he confirmed that it was in the area experiencing the heat, which was why he was drawing more of the energy there. Heat is often experienced when the energy is drawn to a symptom of a physical nature.

## Coolness

This usually suggests a block in the area. Not much energy is able to be received and the corresponding chakra may be malfunctioning. Often, coolness can indicate blocks of an emotional or even a spiritual nature. There may be repressed feelings that are not accessible on a conscious level. The exercise to clear energy blocks in Chapter 6 may help. Deep inner work may be required to release very deep-seated blocks. Treating the whole body will help to free up the energy in this area.

## Tingling

Tingling can indicate the presence of inflammation. If there is no obvious cause of the inflammation, there may be suppressed anger. The knees and jaw often store much anger. Reiki is effective in allowing deep seated feelings to surface and usually the tingling sensation diminishes rapidly.

## Hands Feel Strongly Drawn to an Area

This implies that the energy is much needed in an area. Usually the energy is being freely drawn. Sometimes a longer period of time may pass whilst the hands are in a particular position almost without our awareness of it. This is how it should be. Extra energy is being transmitted where it is required.

## Hands Feel Repelled From an Area

This usually implies that there is an old deep-seated issue that the person is reluctant to face. There is likely to be an energetic blockage in the area that is resisting the energy at all costs. It could even result from a past life trauma. It is important to ascertain whether the client feels ready to deal with such deep-seated blockages. If there is fear, then the person is not ready. It is then best to leave this area alone and perhaps send Second Degree Reiki to help heal the cause and assist the person. Time must be allowed for the healing process to unfold.

### Dull Pain

This often implies that there has been a physical problem in the past, perhaps scar tissue in this area which has caused a build-up of energy. As it is natural for the body to gradually deal with such areas, Reiki will help accelerate that healing process.

### Sharp Pain

This may pinpoint an area where there is a build-up of energy that urgently needs releasing. Concentrating on this area will help to break it down and allow the free flow of energy once more. Whole body treatment is advised, rather than treating this area in isolation, although it may need more focus initially.

### Vibration

This may indicate the chakra has been under- or over-functioning in this area and energy is being drawn through to balance and repair it. Often the person may be totally unaware of the vibration. Alternatively, they may have felt a strong vibration whilst your hands experienced no movement at all. The hands will not be moving in any event. It will be the way in which the energy is moving that is causing the vibration.

It may be confusing when the person's impressions do not coincide with your own and this is because they are processing the experience differently. Their own tension, fear or anger will personalize their experience of the energy and it is of no cause for concern.

The above is a guide only and many healers will interpret their impressions differently, in their own way.

In conclusion the minimum requirements for the Usui System of Reiki at Reiki First Degree include:

A minimum of nine hours tuition
The History
Four initiations or attunements
The hand positions
Treatment of self and others
The five ethical principles

# CHAPTER ELEVEN
# THE SECOND DEGREE CLASS

The second degree class enables the participant to become a channel for a far greater amount of life force energy than at First Degree level. It is recommended that at least three months is taken to assimilate the energy at First Degree level before enrolling for a Second Degree class.

There is usually one initiation at Second Degree level which attunes people to the symbols that are received during this class. A further level of energy is activated at this level and a 21- or 30-day cleanse is again recommended to enhance the integration of this energy.

Following initiation at Second Degree level, the energy flows through the system in greater quantities and when self treating or treating others, just three minutes instead of five will suffice in each position for self-treatment, unless there are circumstances which dictate otherwise, such as in first aid applications. The energy that is transmitted is far more intensive. This is particularly helpful for professional therapists who incorporate Reiki into their treatments and work to a time schedule.

We still recommend an hour when giving a full treatment to another person. There is greater flexibility, knowing that usually within three minutes the person will usually have drawn as much as is needed in any one position, unless there is something specific going on and more energy is required in a particular position.

This course is usually divided into three sessions that can either be held over a weekend or over three evenings. As in First Degree, the format varies with individual Reiki Masters. One session may include the attunement, another the three symbols plus additional information relating to their use and the third session may focus entirely on the absent healing technique and the stronger form of mental and emotional healing. Usually the training is lively and exciting as the material contained at this level is both fascinating and thought provoking.

## Intuition and Second Degree

The third eye, if it has not been sufficiently stimulated at First Degree, will certainly be at Second Degree, increasing perceptive abilities of participants. Some students at this level find they become able to perceive energy fields and auras. Clairvoyance or intuitive abilities may develop. This is because the Second Degree attunement works directly on the etheric body rather than affecting the physical body as at First Degree. As time goes on, it is often easier for a person who has taken Second Degree to receive information at an intuitive level than previously. The connection to the Higher Self is also strengthened by the initiation at this level.

To develop intuition, it is important to be able to differentiate between impulses and inspired intuition received from our Higher Selves. Intuitive thoughts and messages are often accompanied by feelings of peace and harmony. They can be strong or vivid thoughts that do not cause feelings of panic. They usually reoccur **at least three times**. Impulses and desires conversely can evoke a sense of urgency or anxiety, putting one under pressure. They often feel as though they must be carried out without delay. If one is aware and can distinguish between the two, it can be very helpful.

## Reiki Symbols

At this level, three symbols as well as the three mantras which activate them are taught. These are not printed here out of respect for the sacred nature of the information and because they cannot be used until a person has been attuned at this level.

Each of the symbols are learned by heart and committed to memory. Afterwards instruction is given on how and when to use the symbols. There have been many books written about symbols, describing them to be the universal cosmic language.

## Distant Healing

This method allows a person to send healing to recipients who are not physically present. This approach uses symbols and a specific technique to connect with a person or any living thing and send energy to them as if they were in the same room. All that is needed is their name, a picture or perhaps bringing their voice to mind to establish a connection through which energy can be transmitted.

This technique also offers the possibility of being able to send energy to numerous recipients simultaneously. Sometimes, once the connection has been established, it is possible to receive a response as well. We have been told of occurances when a recipient had been in a coma whilst receiving distant healing. It was possible to elicit a meaningful response from that person that was to change the lives of their family and close friends.

It is also possible to transcend time as well as space using the distant healing method. Healing can therefore be sent backwards to a difficult period in one's life or forward to when you will be taking an examination or attending an interview. The results can be extraordinarily effective in bringing harmony to the present.

Absent healing can also be sent to situations as well as living beings and can be transmitted to war zones or disaster areas. Reiki can be sent to situations throughout the world. There is a networking organization called the Reiki Outreach International, founded by Mary McFadyen, an American Reiki Master, which co-ordinates the sending of energy to world situations, so that as much distance healing as possible is sent to a particular area or situation. Reiki Practitioners can access a telephone recording in many countries to find out the current area being focused upon. (See Useful Addresses on page 147). Even weakened groves of trees or gardens can be treated on regular basis as can wild animals, farm animals or domestic pets.

Rooms can be cleansed energetically by using the symbols (see Chapter 7). Offices or kitchens can be treated to minimize the effects of emissions from electrical equipment. It is recommended that appliances connected to the electrical supply should be at least two metres (six feet) away from where you sleep. All electrical equipment should be switched off and unplugged when not in use as well.

Food can be treated to enhance its nutritional content. Raw food contains live enzymes and a high degree of life force energy which is ideal. Cooked and pre-packaged supermarket food carries far less, and benefits considerably from being treated. We recommend Leslie Kenton's *The New Biogenic Diet* (see Further Reading, page 152) and her other books for a high energy diet containing a far greater proportion of unadulterated raw food than is normally consumed. The recipes look and taste marvellous and literally transform your energy levels and your waistline without depriving you of substantial meals.

Surprisingly, energy can even be sent to computers, cars and other machines and it is fascinating to see how faulty equipment can sometimes be seen to respond. All manufactured materials were constructed from organic substances originally and can be treated with the energy, although it would be unwise to depend on the energy for all repairs.

*Beaming Reiki Across a Room*

With Second Degree it is possible to beam the energy from your hands across a room whenever you wish to do so. This can be a useful technique when you wish to send energy when it would not be appropriate to place hands on for any reason.

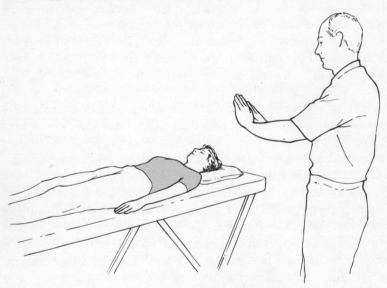

In conclusion, there are many ways in which distant healing can be used, some of which are mentioned above and many others which are covered extensively in our Reiki Second Degree course. Furthermore, distant healing can also be used with clients who are in the same room as yourself who would not be open to a hands-on healing treatment, such as a person undergoing counselling. Distant healing would speed up the counselling process and serve to help the person endure the emotional upheaval that may be surfacing.

## Second Degree and Personal Development

The Second Degree initiate can use the absentee healing technique on himself to heal old situations and pave the way energetically for those yet to come. Much clearing can be done by this method. The person may become more consciously aware having cleared old patterns of response and be more receptive to the awakening, intuitive aspect of himself, as well as having more clarity to deal with the changes that this will inevitably bring.

It often happens that Second Degree initiates have overcome their initial fears and can move forward with a greater sense of wholeness and balance than at First Degree level. There is literally more time available as less time need be spent on self-treatment. There are many tools at the disposal of the initiate with which to shape his or her destiny in the most beneficial way.

It is more important than ever at this stage to decide what you would like to create in your life, how you wish to spend your time, who you wish to be with and which career would bring you the most fulfilment.

Thought is very powerful. Because energy follows thought, we are all constantly creating with our thoughts. Whether it is the evening meal or deciding to enrol on a college course, it always begins with a thought. Betty Shine in her book *Mind Magic* describes the energetic changes that occur when a person entertains negative thoughts. Negative thinking can be draining and limiting. Positive thoughts are self empowering and energizing. Hence holding a negative idea such as illness in the mind, will eventually bring about illness. Conversely, envisage yourself accomplishing whatever you set out to do and you will be successful.

Energy follows thought and before we create anything for ourselves, it always begins with a thought. When we wish to make changes for ourselves, we create thoughts of new possibilities before we take action to bring this about. Energy is also magnetic and tends to attract energy of a similar vibration as we often see in the 'coincidences' that happen to us all on a daily basis. An example of this is the very person we have just been thinking about telephones us unexpectedly that same evening.

Discovering our dreams isn't always easy and may require much effort on our part to bring into reality. Once we clarify our goals however, we have the ability and the tools to bring them into being. Our intentions are very powerful. Dr Deepak Chopra refers to our intent as 'the software of the mind'. All we need to do is to decide what we want.

### The Power of Focus

It often happens in our everyday life that we have so many areas to give our attention to, that we dissipate our energy and as a result lose the power of our focus. We feel drained and exhausted. Second Degree initiates can use the absent healing technique to send Reiki to a number of people or situations at one time. This usually works well though the energy can be less powerful when sent to a large number of recipients at once. It is important to consolidate one's focus of attention. This can be an important step in moving forwards and not becoming stuck from both an energetic and a practical point of view.

One person described suffering from constant exhaustion. She was surprised she didn't have any more energy as her lifestyle was healthy and active. She went on to describe the many commodities and services she offered to others. The list was extensive. It included a dozen therapies, financial advice, picture framing, lecturing, printing, designing, writing, publishing and painting as well as swimming and walking.

She was obviously a very capable, talented person. However, whilst talking about her life, she realized that if she decided to focus on fewer areas, she would conserve her energy and allow herself to progress at a steadier pace. Her energy would be focused in fewer directions, giving her more energy and vitality.

By concentrating one's focus on one or two major areas, it is possible to increase clarity, and form a powerful personal vision that is easier for others to relate to. It's a question of choosing a path and then following it. One is always free to change, and choose a different path. It is difficult to follow all paths, especially at the same time.

Personal growth with Second Degree contains many possibilities and requires our focus and intent to bring about positive change. To be empowered, we need to have control over our lives and over our emotions so that we can enjoy a greater sense of wholeness, harmony and balance.

In conclusion the minimum requirements for the Usui System of Reiki at Second Degree include are:

A minimum of nine hours tuition
One initiation
Three symbols
Three mantras
The use of the symbols especially:
Distance Healing
Mental and emotional healing

# CHAPTER TWELVE
# THIRD DEGREE OR MASTER'S TRAINING

The Third Degree is for those wishing to help others become channels for Reiki energy. It is recommended that anyone wishing to undertake such training should allow a year to pass from the date of their Second Degree training before starting Master's training.

This time is needed to integrate the energies and gather adequate experience of using the material learned at that level, in order to be able to competently assist others to do so later. Additionally, those who give many Reiki treatments increase their own capacity to channel the energy. Therefore a person who practises Reiki at First Degree on a daily basis for ten years will channel more energy than a Second Degree initiate would, when used once a week for six months.

In the Usui System of Reiki, this path is seen as a calling and at the time of Mrs Takata, a person who wished to become a Reiki Master had to give up all that he owned. Dr Usui's students would travel the length and breadth of Japan with him learning about Reiki until Dr Usui felt that the person was ready to be initiated as a Master in his own right.

After the death of Mrs Takata in December 1980, and the subsequent recognition of Phyllis Lei Furumoto as Grand Master, the Usui Masters got together and having shared information about their own training, realized that they had each been taught slightly differently by Mrs Takata. It was felt appropriate to formally agree upon common elements of training for all future Masters to uphold high standards of tuition. They subsequently formed the Reiki Alliance that was to be an organization to both honour the spiritual lineage of the Usui System of Reiki and standardize the way in which it was taught.

Those who wished to teach Reiki were to become an apprentice or under-study to an existing Reiki Master for a minimum of twelve months. Over the years, there have been different approaches. At this time, only senior Reiki Masters who have themselves been teaching for over three years, can initiate other Masters. The principle behind this is, if you haven't the experience of holding classes and guiding students successfully yourself, you can hardly assist others to do so.

Mrs Takata had equated the cost of training as a Reiki Master to the degree of individual commitment of the trainee and charged $10,000 US, a substantial sum in the 1970s. This was for approximately one year's apprenticeship training which ensured the student had all the necessary knowledge and experience to be able to impart it meaningfully to others. This was also to discourage those not fully dedicated to follow such a path. In addition, the cost of training at Second Degree was fixed at $500 US and First Degree at $150 US. These costs remain approximately the same today with some variations depending on the individual Reiki Master and the country in which it is being taught.

The cost of Master's training appears considerable even by today's standards. It must be said that the cost of spiritual and personal growth is difficult to quantify especially in our consumer-orientated culture.

Millionaires cannot go out and buy peace to carry around in their hearts. Additionally, wisdom is not transferable from one person to another. It is not a commodity that can be bought and sold. There needs to be insight and understanding before concepts can be grasped and integrated. Considerable experience is required before we can gain enough perception to assist others on their path. A wise sage cannot compile all his knowledge and understanding into a manual and ask someone else to take his place, because he or she simply wouldn't be able to.

What one is really paying for in this apprenticeship is someone to train you to understand your own processes so clearly that you can shine a torch for others to pave the way for their own journeys. If your own understanding and experience is superficial, limited or misguided, it does not bode well for future students. It may be possible to deceive your training Master, but you wouldn't delude future students for long.

One particular lady telephoned us recently to explain that as she had previously been a school teacher, had taught yoga for 20 years, mastered many other holistic disciplines and a number of philosophies over many years, couldn't we just initiate her quickly as a Reiki Master, as the year's training didn't really seem like 'good value for money' and she needed to spend money on home improvements and repairs. We explained to her that even if she was an explorer who had travelled to dozens of countries, if there was another country that she had never visited, she would never really know what it was like, unless she spent time there to discover its uniqueness for herself.

However it cannot be said that after twelve months or so, infinite wisdom will be yours automatically. Training as a Reiki Master involves achieving a number of objectives, one of which is development of the personality, so that initiates have the necessary tools, maturity and spiritual understanding to guide others. As we are all unique, progress is variable and only time can determine whether a person is competent enough to respond in an appropriate way to meet his future student's needs. As we are all learning on a daily basis throughout our lives, twelve months or so immersed in one's own personal development cannot guarantee that one has evolved sufficiently enough to master one's own inner processes, let alone be in a position to guide others to do so.

It is possible to buy the title of Master, but for those wish to **be** a Master, a high degree of personal responsibility is needed, as well as a correspondingly high level of commitment.

### Traditional Master's Training

For those considering training as a Reiki Master, it is of vital importance to find a teacher that you resonate with, as you will be spending much time with this person and need to establish a good rapport at the outset. It is not expected that this relationship will remain the same throughout the training. It is a learning curve and during the training period there will be times when anger and frustration will surface. This is to be expected as part of the process and will not serve to restrict the training in any way. On the contrary it will allow valuable lessons to be learned. The Reiki Master may also have limitations. He or she is not infallible.

At the end of training, the student may not yet know all the answers. However they should have progressed sufficiently to be thirsting for more knowledge and be willing, flexible and disciplined enough to progress down a path of continuous self-development and spiritual evolvement wherever that may lead. He or she will be able to hold a clearer, personal vision of their own future and have the ability to be able to create it.

We do not know whether the charges for Reiki Master's training will increase, decrease or remain the same in the future. Whilst the Reiki Alliance is in existence, it is likely that high standards of teaching will be maintained by its members. It is probable that whatever the cost, the personal development of the student will enable him or her to sufficiently progress during training, and subsequently to be able to rapidly recoup the initial outlay.

The best part of this training is that it is adapted to suit the needs of the individual and therefore it is not possible to definitively state what may constitute a traditional Master's training.

We have, however, described below what such a training could include on the understanding that certain parts may vary infinitely depending on the needs of each particular student.

Firstly, training would include learning how to attune others to become a channel for the energy. This is an essential part of the training and would include in-depth knowledge on the attunement process.

Additionally, teaching the accompanying material and learning how to hold a successful Reiki class is a fundamental part of training and the student would also need considerable practise before teaching. Tuition would also include detailed knowledge of group dynamics and group energy. Understanding the form of the Usui System of Reiki would also be an important element.

Dealing with one's own transference patterns as well as those of others would constitute an important aspect of training. Those who aspire to teach others would have to ensure they are able to maintain a professional relationship with students with clearly defined boundaries. It is important that ego is kept in check and the shadow side dealt with.

### Shadow Side

When we are very young, we are carefree and spontaneous. We soon realize that we are not the centre of the world and must fit in with other's people's needs. In order to love and be loved, we find later that we are unable to express ourselves as freely and repress some of our instinctive characteristics. Jung termed these suppressed traits our shadow side and warned that unless they are recognized and acknowledged they can be a destructive force in our lives. Deluding ourselves that our shadow side does not exist can lead to our downfall.

An individual's personal development would concentrate on issues appropriate to the student. No less important and perhaps linked to the above is the spiritual development of the student. There would be a considerable amount of inner work for the student during this period.

The need for clarity and understanding of the spiritual and mystical nature of the initiations and the profound changes that can occur, are important aspects of this work. It is also important for the student to understand the limitations of the energy as well and hold a realistic understanding of what it can and cannot do.

Practical assistance and advice will be given to the student in the setting up and running of a successful healing centre. This should include financial and marketing guidelines as well as practice management.

Advice would be given as to the professional conduct of a Reiki Master. Personal, intimate relationships with students or clients are never appropriate, whatever the circumstances.

Organizing workshops, teaching practice and healing are all fundamental parts of training and would involve the student getting as much practise as possible in this area.

Overall, it is important for the student to have a full understanding of the Usui tradition as well as having a good grounding is psychotherapy and esoteric knowledge. To continue the tradition as a Master and impart it to others requires a number of abilities. It is as well to have the stability to hold a high level of energy (without taking yourself too seriously) tempered with some humility and reverence.

# CHAPTER THIRTEEN
# HOW TO FIND A REIKI MASTER

Reiki is easy to learn and there are now Reiki Masters teaching in or near major cities in many parts of the world. Unfortunately, at this present time, there is no regulating body to which all Reiki Masters must belong nor any licensing system in place at the time of writing, which ensures that minimum standards are adhered to.

The demand for Reiki training has risen substantially over the past five years and without compulsory regulation in place, individual enterprise has become the order of the day. Whilst there is some excellent tuition available, it has to be said that training as a whole is variable. However, it is not quite such a minefield if you are willing to invest a short of amount of time and effort to assess whether the tuition offered is of a high standard.

Reiki is an oral tradition and initiations or attunements should be carried out face-to-face with a Reiki Master, usually in a group setting. Anyone offering attunements by mail, telephone, the Internet, a book or even from a different room, is not providing adequate Reiki training and should not even be considered. This is different from sending or receiving absent healing which of course can be sent from across the world.

The size of the group is important as each participant should receive personal attention and support and in very large groups, unless there are a number of Reiki Masters or teaching assistants present, the needs of the individual may be overlooked.

In addition, each level of the Usui System of Reiki should be taught separately with a gap of at least three months between First and Second Degree. There should be a further gap of approximately one year before embarking on a Master's training course with plenty of practical experience of giving treatments in-between.

We are all individual and there is bound to be considerable variation in the way each teacher imparts the same knowledge to students. The methods described in this book cannot represent an exact duplication of the way in which every Usui Reiki Master teaches. It will in essence be representative of a unique energetic form of therapy. It must be remembered that Mrs Takata taught Reiki as an intuitive healing art and not a rigid system as such. However, it must be said that anything that departs too radically from the Usui System of Reiki, simply isn't Reiki. It is something else.

At the time of writing, other energetic forms of healing have been developed over the past few years which have been termed The 'Original Usui System of Reiki' with another name alongside the word Reiki. Some of these include Karuna Reiki, Reiki & Seichem etc. Each has several levels and further initiations. We would like to see them differentiated from Reiki in the future by being taught in their own names and in their own right.

It is confusing for those looking to train in a particular way and finding they are not entirely sure of the tuition they will be receiving. Everybody knows that homeopathy and reflexology are different healing arts by their names. Nobody could possibly mistake one for another.

The Usui System of Reiki is complete in itself and does not require extra initiations or levels to improve or enhance it in any way. It is a system that imparts sacred knowledge and energetic attunement to allow healing ability to be initiated and personal growth to be accelerated both at the time and over a period of many years to come.

From our own experience, the symbols at Reiki Second Degree can be used in such a multitude of ways, it would also seem unnecessary to further complicate what is already a complete healing system.

Whilst discerning the right Reiki Master can appear a daunting task, it is helpful to remember that the best way to find a teacher might be through the personal endorsement of others. Many advertisements only contain the name and date of classes and it is not possible to determine what sort of tuition is being offered. Additionally, the best teachers sometimes never advertise at all. Recommendation is perhaps the best way and where possible, make personal contact with the Master, assess what kind of classes are being offered and then go with your inner feelings, trusting that you are making the right decision. It is far better to wait a little longer for the right teacher, than take the first opportunity offered which 'feels wrong' at the outset.

The Reiki Alliance has a directory which lists traditionally trained Masters based in most parts of the world. It presently has two addresses, one in the US and one in Europe. They can be contacted directly. (See Useful Addresses on page 147.)

The Reiki Association can supply a member's directory of Reiki Masters throughout the UK for a nominal charge. This lists each Master's background, training and experience so that it is possible to narrow down the options available and from a practical viewpoint, determine who teaches in your locality. (See Useful Addresses on page 147.)

# CHAPTER FOURTEEN
# BECOMING A REIKI PRACTITIONER

The only requirement necessary to become a Reiki practitioner is an open heart, the desire to receive the attunements and the intention to use the energy.

Reiki has grown considerably in popularity over the past ten years and there is much demand for practitioners. It will probably be helpful if you intend to practise Reiki on a professional basis if you join a Reiki practitioner's organization in the country you are living in. They will provide valuable contacts with other practitioners and keep you informed of any new developments. The UK Reiki Association also has a referral list of practitioners that could include your entry and allow people requiring treatment to contact you directly.

Before opening your door to clients, it is important to find out if there are any specific laws pertaining to non-medical practitioners where you live, just in case there are regulations you need to be aware of. Your Reiki Master should be able to advise you on this.

*Insurance*

Whereas the Usui System of Reiki in itself is not harmful and only serves to break down the barriers to harmony, it is as well to have insurance, if you are a professional practitioner of any persuasion. Personal indemnity insurance is essential. If you are already practising another healing art, it may be possible to add Reiki to the policy.

Most insurance companies can provide a quotation for this and in many countries there are specialist insurance companies who provide policies especially for those working in the caring professions. It is also recommended that you take out liability insurance to protect yourself from litigation should a person sustain accidental damage to themselves such as falling down the stairs at your home or slipping over whilst getting off the treatment table. If you work at a clinic, they will probably have this insurance already.

## Experience

If you do not feel confident enough, practise more on your family and friends. Take your time. If there is no one you can practise on, find out where your local sharing group is held and practise on other Reiki people there.

If you haven't used Reiki for a long time, ask your Reiki Master if you can sit in again on First Degree and refresh yourself. You may wish to spend some time offering Reiki to people in hospitals or hospices. Often maternity units welcome healers to treat expectant mothers.

Helping demonstrate Reiki at holistic health exhibitions is also a marvellous way to gain the experience of treating many people. It is surprising how much people benefit from treatment at these exhibitions despite the often noisy environment. You may wish to volunteer your services to assist the Master who trained you if they demonstrate Reiki at exhibitions in your area.

## Client Records

It is also recommended that you keep client records for some time, to ensure that details are available should they be required in the future, for any reason however unlikely. These need not be extensive and should ideally include the name, address and telephone number of the person together with their Doctor's address and contact number. Additionally it would be wise to record any medication they may be taking and if they have any artificial aids such as a pacemaker fitted. It is of course never appropriate to ask clients to alter the medication they have been prescribed by their doctor. It would be useful to record the reason for their treatment and if they are or have been treated for any mental or physical disorder of any kind and to note any allergies or phobias they suffer from.

## Confidentiality

Confidentiality is an important part of any professional relationship. If you feel there are certain circumstances where you could not guarantee to maintain confidentiality in respect of your client, if you felt they may harm themselves for example, then this must be mentioned at an early stage.

### When Reiki is Not Appropriate

It is sensible to be aware of when Reiki is not an appropriate treatment. This is covered fully in Chapter 5.

### Advertising

Many of your clients will come to you because they have been personally recommended to do so, which is the best way. To let people know what you do, it is helpful to have some small brochures printed explaining what Reiki is and where you can be contacted. When you have gained sufficient experience and confidence, you may wish to let local holistic centres know that you are a Reiki practitioner and could offer their client's treatments on certain days of the week or when required.

Should you decide to have cards printed with your details, it is advisable not to include your home address. Print your details and telephone number only.

### Treatment Couch

You may have access to a treatment table at a clinic or healing centre or you may decide to invest in one for your own use. There are many options available and it is well to remember that most are designed for massage and are understandably sturdy. It is not necessary to buy such a table for Reiki unless you practise some form of holistic massage. Nor would a table need to be exceptionally wide. Your own comfort is paramount when giving a treatment and you would not wish to be stretching across an unnecessarily large table. It is advisable to find a table that is strong, as light as possible and one that is high enough for you to reach your person without inflicting damage on your own back.

Many tables flatteringly named 'portable' are probably better described as 'luggable'. It is preferable to buy one that you can easily manoeuvre, rather than one that requires a couple of weight-lifters to transport for you. If you can find a table which allows you to pull up a chair at the head and possibly the foot of the table, you may well find this a very useful feature. When treating the head positions especially, it is wonderful to have the option of being seated, resting the elbows comfortably on the table either side of the person's head. At the Reiki School, we have them built especially for us and they are made to order – details of these and others at the back of the book.

*Charges for Treatment*

If you are treating your family only, you will not need to charge, though once you decide to become a professional practitioner, you will need to receive an exchange of energy to cover your costs and pay your own bills.

If you are in a situation where you are helping on a voluntary basis then it may not be appropriate to charge for your time. If you are paying for the use of a room in a holistic centre and incurring costs advertising your treatments, then it would be appropriate to make a charge for your work.

Many practitioners offer a discount if a course of several treatments is booked in advance. It is a sad fact of human nature that people do not appreciate what they receive free of charge. Many practitioners who do not charge, are often less busy and are frequently let down at the last minute, whereas those charging a high price are booked for months in advance and have a waiting list. It could also be that people do not feel comfortable owing an obligation to others that they can never repay.

You may however feel you would like to offer treatment at a concessionary rate to disadvantaged persons such as those who are unemployed or disabled.

*Coping with Emotions*

In a loving, caring environment, it is not unusual to find that clients are able to bring up deep-seated emotion. It is helpful to keep a box of paper tissues in your therapy room for this purpose. Expressing grief, sadness, anger, fear or whatever emotion has been buried, helps to heal pain.

Our culture often encourages us to 'be brave' and 'soldier on' when we would rather allow ourselves to feel vulnerable and acknowledge our feelings. That is why this gradual growth process that accompanies Reiki provides an environment for us and our clients to face their emotions. Only from personal experience and growth in this area can a practitioner provide the empathy, understanding and support to another who, as a result of the Reiki treatment is facing a difficult emotional time.

Providing a safe, loving, supportive environment allows people to shed their tears and release their sadness. Often this outpouring of emotion will herald a turning point in their healing process.

*Some Practical Details for Giving a Reiki Treatment*

- Wash the hands before and after treatment.
- Be sure to remove watches and rings.
- Make sure your breath is fresh – don't eat spicy food before a treatment.
- Use tranquil, meditative music.
- Use the positions as a guide, but act intuitively when placing hands.
- Wear clean, comfortable, light weight clothing preferably in layers, so that you do not become overheated.
- Place the hands on the body without undue pressure.
- Keep the hands away from the nose and throat.
- Breathe away from the person.
- Try to keep contact with the body or the auric field in between positions, as appropriate.
- Warn the recipient they may experience detoxification symptoms.
- Be as relaxed as you can.

# IN CONCLUSION

'The best and most beautiful things in the world cannot be seen, nor touched . . . but are felt in the heart.'

*Helen Keller*

In this book we have attempted to clarify a healing art that is both simple and enigmatic, straightforward yet mysterious. Reiki brings about a subtle inner shift that forever changes the perception of those drawn to it, opening their hearts and minds to infinite possibilities. It is intangible yet can be perceived by the senses. With it, each person can move closer to a state of wholeness and balance.

Overall, Reiki can be said to be a powerful tool for raising self-awareness and enabling us to participate in our own healing process. By leading us to the cause of our own suffering, we are better able to assist others to do likewise.

It can help to uncover aspects of ourselves that we were previously unaware of. Through the discovery of our own qualities and abilities, we are then able to embrace others with more compassion and understanding.

When we reach a turning point in our own lives, the clarity and the increased awareness can help us to determine the next step, so that we are able to respond with love instead of fear and move forward with confidence instead of uncertainty, trusting that things will always work out for the best in the end. Our vision of how our life can be, will create that life. Seeing through present obstacles will take us beyond them.

The healing energy of Reiki could be said to equate to love. Pure unconditional love transcends all barriers and restores equilibrium within the body, mind and spirit and brings joy in its wake.

Life is a song – sing it
Life is a game – play it
Life is a challenge – meet it
Life is a dream – realize it
Life is a sacrifice – offer it
Life is love – enjoy it

*Sai Baba*

# USEFUL ADDRESSES

The Reiki Alliance
PO Box 41
Cataldo
Idaho 83810-1041
USA
Tel: 208 682 3535
Fax: 208 682 4848

The Reiki Alliance
Honthorstraat 41 11
1071 DG Amsterdam
Netherlands
Tel: 31 20 67 19 276
Fax: 31 20 67 11 736

Office of the Grand Master
PO Box 220
Cataldo
Idaho 83810
Tel: 1 208 682 9009
Fax: 1 208 682 9567

The Reiki Association
68 Howard Road
Westbury Park
Bristol B56 7UX
UK
Tel: 01981 550829
Fax: 0117 942 0275

The Reiki School
Budworth
Shay Lane
Hale, Altrincham WA15 8UE
UK
Tel: 0161 980 6453

The Tao of Books
Unit 7 Willow Farm
Allwood Green, Rickinghall
Diss IP22 1LT
UK
Tel: 01379 890190

Airlift Books
Mail Order List
1004 Mollison Avenue
Enfield, Middx EN3 7NJ
UK
Tel: 0181 804 0400
Fax: 0181 804 0044

Planetary Publications
PO Box 66
Boulder Creek
California 950006
USA

LifeRhythm
PO Box 806
Mendocino
California 95460
USA
Tel: 1 707 937 1825

Lotus Light Enterprises Inc.
(Wholesale)
PO Box 1008 RG
Silverlake
WI 53170
USA
Tel: 1 414 889 8501
Fax: 1 414 889 8591

Archedigm Publications
PO Box 1109
Olney
Maryland 20830-1109
USA

## Mail Order Suppliers of Music

New World Music
Paradise Farm
Westhall
Halesworth
Suffolk IP19 8BR
UK
Tel: 01986 782683

Life Tools
23 Buckfast Close
Poynton
Stockport
UK
Tel: 01625 858885

## Music for Reiki Treatments and Relaxing

Steve Halpern    *Spectrum Suite*
Steve Halpern    *Crystal Suite*
Phil Thornton    *Edge of Dreams*
Marcey    *Inward Harmony , Dream Partner, Anthem to Soul, Z, Celestial Dance, Maitreya*
Dr Jeffrey Thompson    *Egg of Time*
Aeoliah    *Angel Love, Angels of Healing Vol. 1*\*
Klaus Weise    *Tibetan Bells* (adapted version – Reiki School\*)
Kevin Kendle    *Distant Horizons*\*
Shad Diamond    *Inside the Crystal*
Denis Quinn (Asha)    *Wings of Fire*
Jim Oliver    *Harmonic Resonance*
Ajad    *Reiki Music vol. 1*\*
Aeoliah    *Healing Music for Reiki 2*\*
Rusty Crutcher    *Love Dance*
Tim Wheater    *Heartland*
Annuvida & Tyndall    *Reiki Healing Hands*
Merlins Magic    *Reiki Light Touch Music*\*
Merlins Magic    *Reiki Music*\*
Rusty Crutcher    *Macchu Picchu Impressions*

\* indicates the music has been especially adapted for Reiki treatments

**Treatment Tables**

The Reiki School
Budworth
Shay Lane
Hale
Altrincham WA15 8UE
UK
Tel/Fax: 0161 980 6453

Magic Flute
PO Box 5614
Eugene OR 97405
USA
Tel: 1 503 686 8878
Fax: 1 503 686 5739

A self-treatment tape is also
available from The Reiki School.

# BIBLIOGRAPHY

Andrea, Steve and Connirae Andreas. *Change Your Mind and Keep the Change*, Real People Press, 1987.

Baginski and Sharamon. *Reiki – Universal Life Force Energy*, Life Rhythm, 1988.

Bodo and Baginski. *The Chakra Handbook*, USA, Lotus Light Publications, 1991.

Brennan, Barbara. *Hands of Light*, New York, Bantam, 1988.

Capra, Fritjof. *The Tao of Physics*, London, Fontana, 1976 and Flamingo, 1982.

Capra, Fritjof. *The Web of Light*, London, Harper Collins, 1996.

Chardin, Teillard de. *The Phenomenon of Man*, London & New York, Collins, 1959.

Chopra, Deepak. *Quantum Healing*, New York, Bantam, 1989.

Day, Jennifer. *Creative Visualisations With Children*, Shaftesbury, Element, 1994.

Dethlefsen & Dahlke. *The Healing Power of Illness*, Shaftesbury, Element, 1990.

Edwards, Gill. *Living Magically*, London, Piatkus, 1991.

Gawain, Shakti. *Creative Visualisation*, New York, Bantam, 1982.

Gerber, Richard. *Vibrational Medicine*, USA, Bear & Co, 1988.

Gibran, Kahlil. *The Prophet*, London, William Heinemann Ltd, 1926.

Haberly, Helen J. *Reiki: Hawayo Takata's Story*, USA, Archedigm, 1990.

Horan, Paula. *Empowerment Through Reiki*, USA, Lotus Light Publications, 1992.

Kingston, Karen. *Creating Sacred Space with Feng Shui*, London, Piatkus, 1996.

Kubler-Ross, Elizabeth. *On Death and Dying*, London, Routledge, 1970.

Levine, Stephen. *Who Dies?* USA, Anchor Books, 1982.

Lubeck, Walter. *The Complete Reiki Handbook*, USA, Lotus Light Publications, 1994.

Lubeck, Walter. *Reiki – Way of the Heart*, USA, Lotus Light Publications, 1996.

Roman, Sanaya. *Personal Power Through Awareness*, USA, H.J. Kramer, 1986.

Roman, S. and Packer, D. *Spiritual Growth: Being Your Higher Self*, USA, H.J. Kramer, 1989.

St James, Elaine. *Simplify Your Life*, USA, Hyperion, 1994.

✓ St James, Elaine. *Simplicity*, London, Thorsons, 1995.

Schwartz, Jack. *Human Energy Systems*, New York, E.P. Dutton, 1980 and Arkana, 1992.

Weil, Andrew. *Spontaneous Healing*, Warner Books, 1995.

Zukav, Gary. *The Dancing Wu Li Masters*, Rider & Co, 1979.

*A Course in Miracles*, Arkana, 1985.

# FURTHER READING

**Reiki**

Fran Brown, *Living Reiki – Takata's teachings as told by*, Life Rythm, USA, 1992.

Paula Horan, *Abundance Through Reiki*, Lotus Light Publications, USA, 1995.

Ursula Klinger-Omenka, *Reiki with Gemstones*, Lotus Light Publications, USA, 1997.

Walter Lubeck, *Reiki for First Aid*, Lotus Light Publications, USA 1995.

✓Brigitte Muller and Horst H Gunther, *A Complete Book of Reiki Healing*, Life Rhythm Publications, 1995.

**Other**

Dr Brian M.A. Alman and Dr Peter Lambrou, *Self Hypnosis: The Complete Manual for Health and Self Change*, Souvenir Press, London, 1993.

✓Richard Bach, *Illusions: The Adventures of a Reluctant Messiah*, Pan, London, 1978.

Chopra, Deepak, *Boundless Energy*, Rider Books, London, 1995.

Paul Coelho, *The Alchemist*, Harper Collins, London, 1993.

Gerald Epstine, *Healing Visualisations: Creating Health Through Imagery*, Bantam, London, 1989.

Louise L. Hay, *Heal Your Body*, Eden Grove Publications, Middlesex, 1989.

✓Louise Hay, *You Can Heal Your Life*, Eden Grove Publications, London, 1988.

Arthur Jackson, *Stress Control Through Self Hypnosis*, Piatkus, London, 1990.

✓Leslie Kenton, *Endless Energy*, Vermilion, London, 1993.

Leslie Kenton, *The New Ageless Ageing*, Vermilion, London, 1995.

✓Leslie Kenton, *The New Biogenic Diet*, Vermilion, London, 1995.

Allegra Taylor, *I Fly Out with Bright Feathers,* C.W. Daniel & Co., 1992.

Neale Donald Walsh, *Conversations with God: An Uncommon Dialogue*, Hodder & Stoughton, London, 1997.

Stuart Wilde, *Affirmations*, White Dove, New Mexico, 1987.

Stuart Wilde, *The Force*, White Dove, New Mexico, 1984.

Stuart Wilde, *Infinite Self*, Hay House Inc., 1996.

Stuart Wilde, *Life Was Never Meant to Be a Struggle*, Nacsom & Sons, Sydney, Australia, 1987.

Stuart Wilde, *Miracles*, Nacsom & Sons, Sydney, Australia, 1983.

**For Children**

Diane Loomans, *Full Esteem Ahead*, H J Kramer, California, 1994.

Diane Loomans, *Positively Mother*, Starseed Press, California, 1991.

Jean Robb and Hilary Letts, *Creating Kids Who Can*, Hodder & Stoughton, London, 1995.

Deborah Rozman, *Meditating with Children: The Art of Concentrating & Centring*, Planetary Publications, California, 1995.

# INDEX

*The New Biogenic Diet* (Kenton)
127
nightmares 85
non-consciousness 29
nose 45, 112
nursing 67
nutrition, *see* diet

offices 127
oil burning 29, 58, 67
openness 99
ovaries 52, 55, 70, 116, 119

pacemakers 62
paediatrics 67
pain 15, 54–5, 57, 124
pain relief 28, 40, 43, 47, 67, 93,
95, 114
pancreas 50, 54, 70–1, 116, 119
parathyroid 48, 114
parents, honouring 110
past:
healing 127, 129
recall 47, 113, 114
peace 29–30, 52–3, 77, 118, 126
personal development 33–5,
99–102, 106, 129–31, 134–6
pets 31–2, 108, 127
pineal gland 45, 46, 71, 72, 112–13
pituitary gland 45, 46, 71, 76,
112–13
plants 32, 127
pleasure 52, 116
positions, *see* hand positions
positive thoughts 129
practitioner, becoming 140–4
pregnancy 83
prevention 28
problem solving 101–2
productivity 46, 113
professional conduct 136, 141
prostate 52, 55, 70, 116, 119
psychotherapy 136
Purse, Jill 74

quantum mechanics 14–16
quartz crystals 77–8
questions 102

Radiance Technique 26
radiotherapy 61
Ray, Dr Barbara Weber 25–6
recall 47, 113, 114
reflexology 66, 112
Reiki Alliance 26, 132, 135, 139,
147
*Reiki and Medicine* (Eos) 65
Reiki Association 139, 140, 147
*Reiki for First Aid* (Lubeck) 57
Reiki Outreach Organization 63,
127
*Reiki Universal Life Energy*
(Baginski & Sharamon) 41
rejuvenation 92
relaxation 29–30, 39, 43, 47, 50,
67, 114, 115
releasing 54, 55–6, 119
repairs 128
reproductive organs 70
resentment 48, 114
respect 110
response, receiving 127
responsiveness 107
room:
beaming across 128
cleansing 87, 127
treatment room 57, 106
rose quartz crystal 78

sacral chakra 70
St James, Elaine 87
scars 67, 77, 124
Second Degree 27, 63, 125–31
security 52, 116
seizures 46, 61, 113
self-awareness 145
self-confidence 88–9
self-criticism 54, 119
self empowerment 34–5